Greenspan's Anguish,

Thoreau As Economic Prophet,
& Other Selected Essays

Greenspan's Anguish,

Thoreau As Economic Prophet, & Other Selected Essays

James Eggert

Green Dragon Publishing
P.O. Box 1608
Lake Worth, FL 33460

Greenspan's Anguish,
Thoreau as Economic Prophet & Other Selected Essays

A Green Dragon Books Publication
First Edition

Green Dragon Publishing
P.O. Box 1608
Lake Worth, FL 33460

Printed in the United States of America and the United Kingdom

ISBN (Paperback) 978-1-62386-000-4

Library of Congress Cataloging-in-Publication Data

Eggert, Jim, 1943-
[Essays. Selections]
Greenspan's anguish, Thoreau as economic prophet, & other selected essays / James Eggert. -- First edition.
pages cm
Summary: "Presents varying economic perspectives and the environmental issues that arise from them"-- Provided by publisher.
1. Economics. I. Title.
HB171.E343 2013
330--dc23
2013026659.

Dedication

To my brother, Richard F. Eggert, —my inspiration into that magical world of ecological consciousness.

Foreword
by Bill McKibben

This is an unusual and valuable book in many respects, its author, is an economist—but not one devoted to the prevailing theology of his profession. Economists mostly work with the dedication of beavers or bees toward the great goals of *More*. Growth, expansion, and acceleration are the sacred words of their creed and they have been enormously successful; their faith has spread around the world, crowding out all other creeds.

And yet there is always something rather, well, dismal about the field. This comes from its disciples' firm determination to wall off certain questions, such as "What makes for happiness?" Or "How do I figure out what I want from life?" They can answer these only pointing to our consumer behavior—we must want what we buy. But they must sense the tautological absurdity of that line of argument.

Now James Eggert, a member of a small school of economists, has begun to think outside the box. And it is curious that he soon delves deeply into a concept long used by his tribe: value. In his essay "Meadowlark Economics," Eggert inscribes it—marvelously—with real meaning, instead of the stale and transactional definition to be found in the front of the Econ textbooks. The meadowlark's "song is pleasing, his color and swoop-of-flight is enchanting."

Suddenly we are using good old nouns and adjectives, the sweet and solid Anglo-Saxon words instead of the ponderous Latinate syllables of the professional journal; these things are valuable, he insists. And if you assign them a value in your heart, then you are in a position to begin to assess both the positives and the negatives of economic growth. For instance the so-called "efficiency" of the modern farm leaves no room for the meadowlarks to nest and fledge their young, is but one of many examples.

This book rambles inefficiently along—which is why it is a good and true book, full of things to talk about with your friends and family, as well as inspiring internal dialogue. There are delightful discussions of craftsmanship, of high jumping and topsoil, of the art of repairing and of many other things that constitute a joyful and complete human life. The essays are lighthearted and smart, and never didactic.

Eggert's book will be of great use to all who read it. It would be especially helpful, though subversive, to give it to anyone you know is an economist. It will help them see, among other things, that grasping onto a one dimensional economic orthodoxy not only shows certain blindness, but can also, unfortunately, turn out to be tragic.

Table of Contents

Grateful Acknowledgement

The nineteen essays in this book have been culled from my earlier collections and on-line sources (see below). Indeed, many of the pieces have been "student-tested," with the goal of introducing college and high school readers to new perspectives on sustainable economics, as well as an attempt to translate the languages of evolution, ethics, and ecology into a framework of everyday economics.

For more general audiences, the book will hopefully stir up discussions, while becoming a catalyst for thinking outside the box and drawing out fresh insights from individuals or perhaps from a reading group. All of the essays have been revised while many have been updated to incorporate the changing global issues, including "The Great Recession" as well as new environmental challenges.

My deepest gratitude to the following publishers:

M.E. Sharpe (James Eggert: *Meadowlark Economics: Perspectives on Ecology, Work, and Learning*, 1992)

William Kaufmann Inc., Mayfield Publishing Company, McGraw Hill (James Eggert: *What Is Economics?* 1st-4th editions)

Ten Speed Press (James Eggert: *Song of the Meadowlark, Exploring Values for a Sustainable Future*, 1999)

Humanics Trade Group Publications (James Eggert: *The Wonder of the Tao*, 2004)

North Atlantic Books (James Eggert: *Meadowlark Economics: Collected Essays on Ecology, Community, and Spirituality*, 2009). Also the North Atlantic Books blog: ("Greenspan's Anguish")

Washington Post Outlook ("Meadowlark Economics," original title: "A Silence of Meadowlarks" and "Deducting Thoreau's Shoes," original title: "Wal-Mart Pond")

Religious Humanism ("Then the Sun Came Up," original title: "The Creationist's Truth," 2004)

PART I
Meadowlark Values

CHAPTER 1

Greenspan's Anguish

"If we take something to be the truth, we may cling to it so much that even if the truth comes and knocks at our door, we won't want to let it in."
—Thich Nhat Hanh

I made a point to save my copy of the Wall Street Journal's October 24th, 2008 edition as an important reminder—a souvenir, if you will—of the Great Recession and its after-effects, but especially those tumultuous years of 2008 and 2009.

There, on the front page is a photograph of a very unhappy Alan Greenspan. The viewer is, I believe, witnessing a moment of anguish—the humbling of a man who apparently had absolute faith in the American free-enterprise system and was a militant proponent of deregulated markets. Indeed, the headline said it all: "Greenspan Admits Errors to Hostile House Panel."

Here was, by many measures, America's most admired economist—an economic "guru" who had navigated the nation through numerous financial storms but had been completely blindsided by the greatest economic crisis of a generation. It was as if Greenspan's free-market, anti-regulation house of cards had come crashing down on top of him, along with the millions of other victims in the US and around the globe.

It was a free fall of not only investments, credit, paper wealth, employment, home ownership, and retirement dreams, but also of an economic orthodoxy where at least one hermetically sealed belief-bubble had burst. It was painful.

I know it hurt because I have been there. First it was a fascination with Classical Marxism; later with Democratic Socialism, while sandwiched in between, an infatuation with Milton Friedman's "Free to Choose" Capitalism. All of them, in their various ways, had turned out to be limited and, in the end, disappointing. Indeed, the long-range fallout from any economic (or other) fanaticism is, as the Buddha pointed out, capable of creating great suffering:

"Aware of the suffering created by fanaticism and intolerance, we are determined not to be idolatrous about or bound to any doctrine, theory, or ideology, even Buddhist ones."

So now I'm wondering: Why not take advantage of this teachable moment? We might begin by jettisoning the standard economic "isms" of the past two centuries as we step out of the rigid, ideological boxes and thus let us distance ourselves from all those "true believers" who have promulgated so many economic and social disasters by trying to cram complex reality into simple ideological molds.

Next, let us invite into our thinking not a new -ism, but a new economic consciousness—a shape-shifting amalgam of market economics informed by ecological principles, community values, and spiritual insights from the wealth of the world's great religions. This perspective I call simply "meadowlark economics."

Markets, of course, do some things very well, including the pricing of relative scarcity or relative abundance of resources, goods, and services. Markets also do well at identifying trade-offs while highlighting the importance of incentives and encouraging genuine entrepreneurs. In addition, markets can "bring forth the goods and services needed for a becoming existence"[1] as one economist elegantly phrased it. Inventiveness and the evolution of sustainable, democratic technologies can also be the fruits of an energized, creative market economy.

But equally important, meadowlark economics will factor in the health of the environment and the maintenance of natural ecological relationships including the integrity of landscapes, the protection of our soils, rivers, lakes, and aquifers, plus the broad spectrum of biodiversity and yes (if we are lucky), the stabilization of Earth's climate.[2]

The health of local communities should also be a touchstone for economic decision making. We might ask for example: how does a new Farm Bill or Energy Bill support local food and transportation systems or encourage livable neighborhoods (vs. the damage done to communities by unregulated "free" trade agreements)?

Finally, the wisdom and insights from the great spiritual traditions should be added to the mix of an ever-evolving economic consciousness. Consider, for example, the movement to promote environmental stewardship (Care of Creation) or the movement to redress the savage disparities of wealth and privilege versus powerlessness and poverty.

As I glance once more at the photo of Alan Greenspan's anguished face and recall other proponents of inflexible economic orthodoxies, I humbly suggest: Please, no more rigid fundamentalism; instead, let us choose a new and expansive economic consciousness leading to a sustainable and healthy future for the Earth, for our children and for our grandchildren.

CHAPTER 2

Meadowlark Economics

"By the power of our imagination we can sense the future generations' breathing with the rhythm of our own breath or feel them hovering like a cloud of witnesses. Sometimes I fancy that if I were to turn my head suddenly, I would glimpse them over my shoulder."
—Joanna Macy

Considering the problems we face in our immediate and long-run futures, and the slow evolution of economic values we're seeing in response, I sometimes wonder about the relevancy of my fellow economists. Among our shortcomings is our limited understanding of the many ecological consequences of our economic decisions.

Ecology and economics have the same prefix, eco-, from the Greek *oikos*, which literally means "household." The original definition of economics therefore implied a careful stewardship of household resources, whereas ecology compels us to try to understand and appreciate the interrelationships within nature's "household." I believe these two households are becoming more interdependent and their futures more and more intimately linked. When we fail to calculate ecological values or see the connections, we pave the way for losses that are both unintended and unwanted.

One example (on a small scale, to be sure) is occurring in and around our dairy farming region of the upper Midwest. We are losing our meadowlarks!

Those of us who walk, bike, or jog along our rural roads enjoy the few meadowlarks that are left. Their song is pleasing, their color and swoop-of-flight enchanting. The complete disappearance of meadowlarks would, plain and simple, be ethically wrong, and would also diminish the quality and richness of our lives.

Why are we losing our meadowlarks? The most likely explanation involves farmers moving to a more efficient haying method called "haylage." Today farmers tend to "green-cut" their hay much earlier in the spring for the purpose of maximizing feed value. Years ago, most farmers let their hay grow longer—perhaps two to three weeks longer—before cutting the hayfield. It was then dried and raked into windrows before baling. This method gave the field-nesting birds (such as the meadowlarks, bobolinks, and dickcissels) sufficient time to establish a brood and fledge their young before the mower arrived on the scene.

Haylage, in turn, is an offshoot of improved farm "efficiency," of substituting machinery and fossil fuels for labor, and of minimizing time and costly rain delays that characterized the old cutting/drying/baling method. These changes took place with the blessings of agricultural economists, university researchers, and ultimately government agencies. But in the meantime, who was valuing the meadowlarks?

Despite their sweet song, these birds have no voice economically or politically. They represent a "zero" within our conventional economic accounting system (we don't even buy birdseed or build birdhouses for meadowlarks). Their disappearance would not create even the tiniest ripple in the Commerce Department's spreadsheets that are supposed to measure our standard of living.

In truth, there are meadowlark values (as opposed to strict monetary values) everywhere—in estuaries and sand dunes, in wetlands and woodlands, in native prairies and Panamanian rain forests. Quite probably the quality of your own life is, to some degree, dependent on these values. They are on every continent; they can be seen upstate and downstate. Just look around and you will find them (like our meadowlarks) on your road, or next door or perhaps in your own backyard.

Meadowlark values are underrepresented in the clear-cutting of old-growth forests to maximize short-run profit. They are certainly underrepresented when politicians attempt to open up the Arctic

National Wildlife and exploit the tar-sands of Canada or when they drill deeper and deeper for oil in the Gulf of Mexico.

Meadowlark values were shortchanged when economists pointed out that the 2010 BP oil spill temporarily increased the gross national product by pouring billions of dollars into the cleanup effort and by paying off fishermen and other affected businesses.

Perhaps it is time we economists begin to rethink our strict adherence to dollar and GDP values. We should not, of course, discard our traditional skills and tools of analysis such as: the importance of pricing, respecting the power of incentives and pointing out trade-offs, or evaluating policies to mitigate poverty and the ravages of recessions. But we also must broaden ourselves to seriously try and incorporate ecological thinking and ecological values along with market thinking and market values—a true “Meadowlark Economist” if you will.

And why not encourage other professions to follow suit? What about a “Meadowlark Engineer,” or a “Meadowlark Politician,” a “Meadowlark Lawyer” or, in regards to grassland birds, a “Meadowlark Farmer?”

I’m ashamed to admit that I took my first elementary class in ecology after teaching economics for more than two decades. I still have a way to go. In addition, I am now beginning to appreciate some of the earlier economics writers, who represent this broader approach to the economics discipline: Ken Boulding, Hazel Henderson, Herman Daly, Lester Brown and E.F. Schumacher, to name a few.

In addition, I hope that more prominent economists of today will feel comfortable not only with traditional market/growth economics, but will also know something of ecological relationships, and will value the integrity of the environment along with the bottom line: economists who will know how to promote development, but will also know how to protect the standard of living of the other organisms with whom we share the planet.

Perhaps future economists will devise, like today’s Environmental Impact Statement (EIS), something that might be called the GIS, or “Grandchild Impact Statement.” This is vital to ensuring that our kids and their kids will have sustainable quantities of biological and other resources, helping to preserve our soils and waters, our fisheries and forests, whales and bluebirds—even the tiny toads and butterflies—so that these entities will have their voices represented too.

So to all CEOs, National Association of Business Economists, government advisers, bankers and media owners, and yes, teachers too: let's dedicate ourselves to a new standard of Meadowlark Economics, protecting and sustaining a larger a more expansive and comprehensive set of durable values for the future.

CHAPTER 3

What's Wrong with Capitalism?

"A Thing is right when it tends to preserve the integrity, stability, and beauty of the biotic community. It is wrong when it tends otherwise."
—Aldo Leopold

Despite its materialistic virtues, something's amiss in the Land of Capitalism. In addition to equity and justice issues, there is also a destructive quality in capitalism that often violates the ecological laws that can and should ensure life's beauty, balance, its health and long-term continuity.

To search for that undermining quality, let us pretend for a moment that you could literally pick up market capitalism as if it were a flawed gemstone. Now place that stone in the palm of your hand and, turning it over and over, inspect the gem for defects, fissures, and possible flaws. First, what would be the economist's perspective? Now angle it slightly differently. What would be the viewpoint of an ecologist? And finally, is it possible to look at capitalism from a prairie's perspective, or say that of an old-growth forest?

ECONOMIST'S PERSPECTIVE

Economists do acknowledge capitalism's imperfections, often describing these defects as "market failures." These include the many unintended impacts ballooning up beyond regular business costs into what are called "externalities," where both consumer behavior and profit-making may have harmful spillover effects that all too often damage human health and landscapes, degrade water and air quality, endanger plant and animal species and possibly, over time, alter the vary stability of Earth's climate. What's the remedy?

Corrective measures will most likely require government intervention to scientifically verify damages. This is necessary to initiate tax policies such as a "health" tax on cigarettes and a "green" tax on harmful emissions. It is also necessary to set more precise standards on pollutants like automobiles, coal-fired power plants, and municipal water supplies, etc., and/or for the enforcement of strict energy efficiency standards (lightbulbs, refrigerators, air-conditioners, etc.). These are just a few examples of environmental regulations that have generally been accepted by the public in most industrial countries. Other areas of intervention include the trading of pollution credits and the enforcement of endangered species laws, as well as negotiating global environmental agreements (whaling, chlorofluorocarbons, CO_2, etc.) enforced by protocols, regulatory oversight, and international law.

Conceptually, all of these measures can be understood in the context of motivating businesses and consumers to pay the full, direct and indirect costs of their economic activity, including the costs of collateral damages to natural and human environments. Simply put, it's a fairness issue—playing the "capitalist game" fair and square. Let's take a minute to examine a way the "economist's perspective" would, hypothetically, tackle a common urban pollution problem, childhood asthma.

According to the Physicians for Social Responsibility (PSR), the number of childhood asthma attacks is on the increase and at least to some degree, these attacks are exacerbated by truck and automobile pollution, including elevated ground-level ozone. Thus, armed with the PSR data, I approached a friend who was a state lawmaker asking if he would consider initiating a modest increase in our state's gas tax (say, one cent per gallon) earmarked not for the usual highway construction and maintenance, but to try to mitigate the damages and costs of urban pollution, perhaps even to reimburse families for asthma-related expenses. I told the representative that I was upset because I was paying too little for my gas; indeed, from an economist's perspective (and moral perspective as well) we should all be disturbed that we were not paying our fair share of the spillover effects of our driving. Put another way, I asked him, "Why do we force families with chronically sick children to subsidize an artificially low-cost transportation system?" An increase in the federal and/or state gasoline tax would be a good beginning—a step towards a fair, full-cost accounting to help pay for the expensive health cost side-effects of automobile transportation.

Any increase in fuel prices, whether through market forces or a pollution tax will indeed create some hardships for drivers, but there will be other benefits too, including cleaner air and, as economists predict, fewer traffic deaths and injuries. Also with higher gas prices, there will be greater incentives to invest in biking and walking trails. Indeed, walkers and bikers in some cities have already pressured local governments to promote more walkable and bike-friendly neighborhoods. Whereas Atlanta is infamous for its un-walkability, Portland, Oregon is at the other extreme with some sixteen pedestrian districts where street design, sidewalks, and traffic laws give the pedestrian priority. Additionally, in Davis, California, bikers enjoy safe, dedicated bike lanes on most city streets. Moreover, developers in Davis are required to provide bike access to new residential and commercial development.

A pollution tax would also encourage more carpooling and, if available, greater use of public transit. Not only would urban children breathe easier, but trees and wildlife would as well, while in the long run it would also reduce CO_2 emissions and help stabilize the climate. And finally, if truckers and automobile owners paid their full direct and indirect costs, it would begin to reduce road congestion while diminishing the political pressure to widen roads and highways, thus minimizing damage to local communities and to the landscape.

Of course, this economists' perspective—even with good science, economic logic, and sensible remedies on its side—is usually no match for well-funded special interest groups. In the case of increasing gas taxes for legitimate spillover costs, the powerful highway, oil, and automobile lobbies will often block legislation that would, as they see it, "harm their industries." Indeed, in response to my gas tax suggestion, my politician-friend told me, "I understand your point, and yes, I agree with you," but then added, "Jim, you'd better forget about it. Politically it ain't going to happen."

ECOLOGIST'S PERSPECTIVE

I dream of a day when parents, politicians, economists, CEOs, bankers, mining and logging companies, and others make their decisions based upon an authentic ecological consciousness, including an understanding and full appreciation of a broad spectrum of environmental values that allow ecosystems to be sustainable, healthy, and whole.

As an example, consider the issue of logging in an old-growth forest, such as the very few that still exist in the U.S. In what ways would the ecologists' perspective differ from that of a for-profit capitalist? To answer this question, I find it helpful to picture in my mind an image of a playground teeter-totter that has a basket at each end. One basket represents strict capitalist, for-profit values and the other represents the universe of ecological values. Now pretend that you were placing weights that represent the different set of values in each of the baskets. What would you place into the Capitalist's Values Basket?

Benefits might include:

- The monetary value of wood products (including export earnings); incomes for loggers, truckers and sawmill workers.
- Increased sales for equipment, including manufacturing jobs.
- An increase in each of these companies' short-term profits.
- A short-term increase in corporate stock prices, adding value to stockholder portfolios.

Importantly, from a for-profit point of view, there would be pressure to maximize all of these values in the short-run by clear-cutting the forest.

Now turning our attention to the other side (ecological values), what representative weights would you put into the Ecological Values Basket?

In some old-growth forests, such as the Menominee Indian Reservation in Wisconsin, the tribe has been engaged for many years in logging, which provides some modest economic benefits while also maintaining their forest's original ecological makeup generation after generation. The Menominee remove a relatively small portion of the forest each year using sustainable management principles which, in turn, incorporate selective cutting based on cultural constraints laid down by tribal elders over a hundred years ago. With this selective cutting strategy, there is some monetary value gained from lumber, logging, sawmill jobs, and some export profits. The return in the short-run is modest compared to clear-cutting, yet over many years, income would be relatively stable.

In addition to these long-term economic benefits, you might now add the following weights representing a broader array of ecological, scientific, and spiritual values:

- A habitat for endangered plants and animals.
- The maintenance of "living classroom" enabling students and scientists to study a healthy ecosystem.
- A source of beauty, inspiration, and spiritual sustenance.
- Healthier rivers, streams, springs (compared to a clear-cut forest).
- Old growth forests protect and create new topsoil, prevent excessive run-off of rainwater and helps recycle nutrients more efficiently than clear-cut forests.
- Old-growth forests sequester atmospheric carbon which helps stabilize Earth's climate.

Tropical old-growth forests, in turn, can provide a sustainable supply of nuts, berries, valuable barks, tubers, mushrooms, and plant-medicines for those who know how to find them. From an ecological perspective, these forests are, in a sense, rolling up their sleeves as they work hard to provide invisible, yet important benefits, or so-called ecological services based on the productivity of the forests' intrinsic natural capital.

When we compare the weights on one side with the other, the Ecological-Values Basket should easily outweigh the Capitalist-Values Basket. Yet, in our current global economic environment involving ultra-powerful forces of profit, propaganda, political corruption, and an obsession with unfettered free trade, we find that the Capitalist Basket almost always wins out. It's as if the global economy were defying gravity as well as other vital laws of nature.

THE PRAIRIE'S PERSPECTIVE

If I were asked to pick an analogy from which we could learn some essential principles for a future economy, my choice would be a native prairie ecosystem that I walk by nearly every day. Some, of course, might think the analogy a little odd, it's not exactly global free-market capitalism, but more a living example of what might be called local natural capitalism. Indeed, this prairie has become a mentor for me, as if it were trying to teach its lessons to a slow-learning, yet earnest economics student. Over the years, I've discovered that this flowering grassland is not only attractive but exceptionally diverse and, like a model sustainable economy, remarkably productive—turning sunbeams, minerals, and carbon dioxide into biotic beauty and eventually converting its plant material into rich, deep, loamy soils.

In addition, this prairie ecosystem has achieved something quite amazing: an exquisite balance between life and death—humming along year after year in a kind of steady-state "economic" efficiency. The prairie recycles virtually everything and unfailingly blooms anew, spring after spring and every summer too!

Prairies are resilient in severe drought, yet they can also handle a week of drenching rain. Moles, monarchs, and meadowlarks survive there. Blue stems and Indian grasses live in prairie too, and so do black-eyed susans, purple prairie clovers, stiff goldenrods, and late summer blooms of purple blazing-stars.

Sometimes I enjoy lying down in the prairie, accepting gravity as it were, my back stretched out along the rough ground, my eyes taking in sunlight, clouds, flowers, seedpods—and there high above, tufts of grasses bending down and up, up and down, as if there were an invisible ocean of windblown waves.

So one might ask, "what direction and what trajectory can we follow toward a more natural, more balanced capitalism?" Can meadowlark values readjust and redress capitalism's spillover effects and correct its corrosive externalities?

Can we conserve—as if an ecological consciousness were our second nature—our planet's plants and animals, it's grasslands, soils, ancient forests, subterranean waters, it oceans, rivers, and reefs?

Like the native prairie, can we find a more harmonic, natural equilibrium that abounds in beauty, balance, and biodiversity? And finally, can we utilize renewable energies and make our economic production more durable and fully recyclable while preserving Earth's realms of amazement and it landscapes of surprise?

CHAPTER 4

Henry Thoreau as Economic Prophet

"In proportion as [a person] simplifies his life, the laws of the universe will appear less complex, and solitude will not be solitude, nor poverty poverty, nor weakness weakness."
—Henry Thoreau

Henry David Thoreau, the nineteenth-century writer and naturalist, was clearly a pioneer of meadowlark values in the field of economics. Indeed, as a professional economist, I have become more and more convinced that this nineteenth century writer was truly a prophet for our time, worthy of the ranks of the major economic philosophers such as Adam Smith, David Hume, Thomas Malthus, and David Ricardo. Let's therefore take a moment to explore some of Thoreau's ideas in more detail.

Consider, for example, the severe housing crisis of The Great Recession, where many Americans found themselves dangerously overextended who had acquired "too much house," and had generally taken on too much debt. Many of these families have been stuck with property that they are unable to sell, or may be threatened by foreclosure while others have already lost their home. Though Thoreau did not specifically predict this particular problem (in his era, it was the overextended farmer that concerned him most), he did make an observation that now seems eerily prophetic. Thoreau warned of the problem of overabundance and that our possessions can, at times, "be more easily acquired than got rid of."[1] Change the description slightly (from "barn" to "home") in the following passage from *Walden* and see how Thoreau's memorable image has a surprisingly contemporary ring to it: "How many a poor immortal soul have I met well-neigh crushed and smothered under its load, creeping down the road of life, pushing before it a barn seventy-five feet by forty, its Augean stables never cleansed..."[2] Thoreau had sympathy for those of us who have too much, whose over-abundance turns out to be more of a problem than a solution.

But if material possessions do not represent "the good life," what does? Might it come from the advance of technological conveniences?

No doubt that Thoreau marveled at and benefitted from many of the byproducts of the industrial revolution. He admitted to the advantages of shingles, sawn-boards, bricks, and especially glass windowpanes ("doorways of light...like solidified air!"[3]) in the construction of his cabin on the shores of Walden Pond. Later in life, Thoreau purchased a spy-glass to better see the birds. Also, as a part-time surveyor and pencil-maker, Thoreau undoubtedly valued the various tools of these professions. But for the most part, he felt that inventions tended to be nothing more than "improved means to an unimproved end,"[4] or even more serious from the viewpoint of living the good life, our technologies are simply "pretty toys which distract our attention from serious things."[5]

At worst, a particular technology could be greatly destructive. Consider the famous quote from *Walden*, "...but though a crowd rushes to the depot, and the conductor shouts 'All Aboard!' when the smoke is blown away, and the vapor condensed, it will be perceived that few are riding, but the rest are run over."[6]

Who cannot recognize the chilling prophesy when we consider the potential for death and destruction with our weapons of mass destruction, or with a catastrophic leak at a chemical factory or a large-scale radiation release as in the Ukraine's 1986 Chernobyl meltdown or Japan's Fukushima reactor accident in 2011?

Or consider the giant machines that are used to devour hundreds of square miles of landscape in the pursuit of minerals or clear-cut trees, or perhaps reshape acres of farmland for roads, suburban developments, or mile after mile of box-stores and strip-malls. "But lo!" Thoreau wrote, "men have become tools of their tools."[7] This kind of economic "progress" that ravages the environment would have been especially distressing to Thoreau, as he believed that there simply could not be a good life, nor even a completely healthy life, without access to nature.

Experiencing solitude in the natural world would therefore play an important role in healing the stresses and depressions of contemporary life where in Thoreau's words: "there can be no very black melancholy to him who lives in the midst of nature and has his senses still."[8] Along the same line (and also foreshadowing the relatively new discipline of environmental psychology), Thoreau wanted us to enjoy the "tonic" of immersing ourselves in a genuine wilderness experience:

"We need the tonic of wildness—to wade sometimes in marshes where the bittern and the meadow-hen lurk, and hear the booming of the snipe; to smell the whispering sedge where only some wilder and more solitary fowl builds her nest, and the mink crawls with its belly close to the ground."[9]

Picture now the thirty-four year old Henry David Thoreau standing before the Concord Lyceum in the spring of 1851 and opening his lecture with: "I wish to speak a word for Nature, for absolute freedom and wildness," and ending with the oft-quoted, "In wilderness is the preservation of the world."[10]

Thoreau's audience must have found these ideas rather strange since there was an immense area of pure wilderness still existing on the North American continent at the time. Today it's not so difficult to understand that Thoreau's passion for wilderness values and the preservation of America's wild spaces was, indeed, a truly prophetic idea.

Thoreau wished that we might value our natural environment and work hard to preserve it against inevitable encroachments. But what else did he advocate? What would he recommend for individuals to improve their private lives?

His answer was as profound as it was brief: "Simplify, simplify!" To exaggerate his point, he advised his readers to "keep your accounts on your thumbnail."[11] More realistically, Thoreau advocated reducing our economic needs, that is, engage in a kind of voluntary poverty or "comfortable frugality." His greatest skill, he once remarked, has been "to want but little."[12] Is this another prophetic notion? Perhaps so, especially when we consider the sooner or later, those of us in the economically "advanced" countries will be forced into lifestyles requiring less and less use of energy and natural resources.

If Thoreau were alive today, he would be appalled by our tremendous private and public debt as well as our growing dependence upon the myriad of specialists who reduce our capacity for doing things for ourselves. He would be advocating for greater local economic production, as much as was practical. He suggested that we might learn to grow our own food as well as build our own homes. For recreation, instead of costly prepackaged commercial experiences (shopping, video games, watching movies, visiting Disneyland, etc.), Thoreau would suggest we simply take a walk in the spirit of adventure, as if it were going on a pilgrimage—"of sauntering toward the Holy Land" as he described it in his essay "Walking."[13] Thoreau would not only be entertained and educated by his excursions, but would often make notes of his observations for his journals, essays, and future books.

Therefore if, in these and other ways, we could advance toward that simpler life which our Concord economist suggests, wouldn't our feeling of economic inadequacy lose some of its sting, the threat of inflation or unemployment lose some of the terror? Wouldn't our feverish anxiety over economic growth diminish? And, in general, wouldn't life itself be more pleasant if we could slow down and become less serious in our striving for The American Dream of luxury and comfort? Thoreau honestly felt that, with some readjustment in our expectations, we might view human existence in a more positive light: "In short, I am convinced, both by faith and experience, that to maintain one's self on this earth is not a hardship but a pastime, if we will live simply and wisely…"[14]

Thoreau, as economic prophet, asks us to reexamine our basic economic premises. Our traditional goal of striving for high material consumption may well carry with it an unexpected price tag in the form of unpleasant complexities, stresses, and anxieties.

Thoreau's objective instead would be freedom; or better yet, what he simply called life: "The cost of a thing is the amount of what I will call life which is required to be exchanged for it immediately or in the long run."[15]

For many contemporary economists, this is indeed an odd theory of wealth, but one truly consistent with the values that promote both personal growth and ecological health—values that Thoreau would defend both in his writings and in the way he lived. Indeed, it is a perspective that would force us all to look at our own lives and the larger economy in a new way, not as gross domestic product per capita, but something like gross domestic life per capita, if that could somehow be measured.

Thoreau was genuinely concerned for the welfare of his readers and fellow citizens. He wished that we would take the time to simplify our lives while deepening our enjoyment of the natural wonders in front of us and around us—and not wake up one morning, late in life, only to discover that we had never really lived.

CHAPTER 5

The Ideal Boss

"Where other companies speak of a supervisor or foreman,
IBM speaks of an assistant...
He is to be the 'assistant' to his workers.
His job is to be sure that they know their work and have tools.
He is not their boss."
—Peter Drucker

As we continue to explore meadowlark values, we might want to take a moment to consider the human ecology of the workplace, especially the important worker/supervisor relationship. If you are like me, you've probably thought about the question, "What are the qualifications for an ideal boss?" This individual might be a supervisor in a business, the armed forces, or perhaps in a university or government agency. Since supervisor and boss have connotations which do not always fit the ideal, let's use instead the softer term facilitator, a designation less hierarchical, more plastic and therefore more open to creative interpretation than the conventional terms.

What should our model facilitator do or not do? What are his or her functions within the organization, and how does this person differ from the traditional boss of today? Undoubtedly every business writer has his or her own twenty-first century lists of skills and competencies needed to become an "effective" leader; for my ideal, let me suggest the following four characteristics.

GARDENER:

I use this term because gardeners, especially home-based organic gardeners, see their present activity in terms of the long-run. Like the characters in an ancient Chinese fables, gardeners look for a payoff far into the distant future. They prepare their soil for years ahead, being aware of long-term nutrient cycles. Gardeners begin gathering materials in the form of old hay, kitchen scraps and manure to make compost that may not break down for a year or two. Once the compost is added to the soil, they may not see results until much later.

In addition, most gardeners seem to enjoy the art of experimenting and, indeed, they don't get too upset if projects sometimes fail. They're anxious to try new varieties, different ways of planting, and novel ways to build topsoil—things that add interest and excitement and offer the experimenter something to look forward to.

FACILITATOR-AS-GARDENER:

The facilitator-as-gardener views his or her operating unit in a similar way—with the goal being the long-term success of the enterprise and the well-being of the workers. The facilitator should offer encouragement, praise, and opportunities for individual development, knowing that these actions may not have a payoff immediately, but will nurture happier, more loyal, and more productive workers for the long run.

Using the gardener as a model, the facilitator should also encourage experimentation and expect some failure, for this is what makes the job interesting and creates possibilities for true innovation. This role is perhaps the most satisfying, for it offers the greatest potential for making lasting improvements.

INTERVENER:

Of all the characteristics, this one comes closer to the conventional idea of a traditional boss. The head of a unit must communicate the larger objectives or mission of the organization to the workers. Combined with this duty, he or she has the responsibility to intervene in those cases in which a worker disregards the goals as defined by the hierarchy. Judgments must be made quickly when such behavior seems likely to threaten the reputation or effectiveness of the unit. Nothing is more demoralizing to the rank-and-file staff than when the unit's reputation wanes and others begin to view the group with diminishing esteem, particularly when the problem lies with just one individual. Such a problem can often be solved by one's coworkers, but when that fails, the facilitator must intervene or the end result may well be more control and regimentation imposed by the hierarchy.

This kind of intervention involves an immense amount of tact, plus an ability to criticize and persuade the individual to change his or her actions without permanently damaging the worker's sense of self-worth. If the one-to-one intervention doesn't work, one must then sound out the staff for their suggestions for handling the situation. In extreme cases, psychological help may be in order but as a last resort, there may be no choice but to fire the worker. Whatever the solution, the facilitator needs to handle this delicate situation with skill and diplomacy. It is, as many readers know, not an easy job.

RESOURCE PERSON:

The third function is that of resource person, a quality that many traditional supervisors often find difficult to learn. As a model, let me suggest the once-common role in healthcare industry: a hospital administrator's relationship to doctors and nurses. Within this medical setting, the administrator is not the boss of the doctor, but more a servant. He or she regards the physicians as professionals who know best how to do what are doing. The hospital or clinic administrator is hired to take care of details such as patient records, equipment purchasing, billing, and marketing the hospital's services to the public. An administrator in this role becomes a true facilitator when they, for example, make a habit of visiting doctors and nurses asking questions such as "What can I do for you?" or "How can I make your job easier?" Although this approach may sound logical, how often do we hear such kind and helpful words from our traditional supervisors?

The main thing to keep in mind is that the facilitator will always regard their employees as experts in their respective field, who will, from time to time, need extra services or resources that only someone in a "higher" position can provide. I see no reason why this helpful role cannot be applied in the executive suites of General Motors, in the administration of a university, an army, or government department, or even between worker and foreman on an assembly line.

LOBBYIST:

In all large organizations, it is not unusual to find fierce competition between departments and divisions for scarce resources. The resources are usually thought of in terms of salaries and staffing. But they might also include other benefits such as the quality of the workplace, access to policy-making, work flexibility, and other tangibles and intangibles that are conferred by the organizational hierarchy.

Therefore an effective facilitator should learn a little of the art of politics and public relations. There will be time when the lobbyist role demands strong representation, especially when the survival of the unit is in question. On such occasions, the facilitator must know how to negotiate effectively and to defend with skill and determination the vital interests of his or her unit. They must know how to deal with subtle power plays of other who may be out to destroy or gain unfair advantage. In such times, good facilitators must convince the hierarchy that their workers are not only making short-term contributions to the larger organization, but are working toward long-term objectives as well.

Of course, this kind of activity can be an especially unpleasant affair. One may find it necessary to make friends with people they neither like nor respect. Unfortunately some individuals in this role may feel the need to overlook illegalities or misrepresent balance sheets or keep quiet concerning dangerous products or knowingly pollute the environment. Such unethical actions will often catch up with the person in question—first on a personal and moral basis, then with his/her organization, and finally, publicly.

When this happens, they jeopardize the morale and possibly the survival of the department or, at the very least, will destroy the progress that had taken years to build up as a resource person and "gardener." When one engages in such questionable activities, it is essential that the workers themselves act as the interveners or "whistle-blowers," first privately, then publicly if necessary.

Yet, if the lobbyist function is performed honestly and well, there can be no better payoff than to have their staff respect their "ideal boss"—whereas this respect, in turn, makes their other roles that much easier in nurturing a healthy environment for the present and future well-being of all concerned.

CHAPTER 6

Less-Dependent Workers

"Avert the danger not yet arisen."
—Vedic proverb

Unemployment is perhaps the most tragic of capitalism's recurrent problems. Idle workers, whether in the Great Depression or the more recent Great Recession, not only diminish the quantity of potential goods and services, but as we all know, to be unemployed for any length of time can also be a protracted nightmare for those afflicted.

Part of our fear of unemployment is due to the fact that we are exposed to an unnatural dependency upon the larger economy and that our livelihood—no matter how competent we may be—is no longer within our control. Economists, with all their theories and recommendations, seem to have no reliable solution to the problem. The best they can come up with is to push for policies that promote national growth via macroeconomic measures such as lowering interest rates, additional government spending and/or tax cuts which may help eventually, but in the short-run feel as remote from the personal lives and personal power of the unemployed as was the original cause of their suffering.

It was while thinking about unemployment in these terms that I came across a couple of interesting readings which started me thinking about the possibility of microeconomic approaches to temporary unemployment. The first was from Norman Ware's 1959 book, *The Industrial Worker,* 1840-1860. In his introduction Professor Ware makes a surprising observation concerning the psychic security of the early American industrial works, before the advent of the monolithic factory system. Ware explains:

"To the worker the security of his tenure seemed greater under the older conditions of production, largely because the tenure of the mechanic and artisan was less dependent upon a single function that was the operative who succeeded him. This is seen most clearly in the case of the Lynn shoemakers how in the early years were able to weather repeated depressions in their trade because they were more than shoemakers. They were citizens of a semi-rural community. Each had his own garden, a pig, and a cow... The more highly industrialized this community became the more completely the worker was divorced from these subsidiary sources of livelihood, the unemployment became a specter where it had once some of the characteristics of a vacation." [1]

And later, Professor Ware amplified his point:

"Before the appearance of the greatly dreaded permanent factory population, bad times had few terrors for the mill operatives. They simply returned to the farms from which they came, welcoming the holiday, and suffering no ill effects from unemployment..." [2]

One might pause a minute to ponder Ware's surprising conclusions that before the advent of the large-scale factory system, unemployment had, as noted above, "some of the same characteristics of a vacation," or that a layoff was often welcomed like a "holiday."

We cannot help but contrast this easy-going, independent lifestyle with the unemployment of today which, more often than not, takes the form of psychological violence, increasing the likelihood, as numerous studies show, of depression, divorce, cardiovascular disease, even auto accidents and suicides.

This leads to the question: Is it possible to modernize the earlier (pre-industrial) strategies for coping with today's unemployed? How far can we today take the empowerment model described by Professor Ware that characterized semi-independent self-reliant workers, but apply it to today's economy?

A couple of strategies include preparing oneself with do-it-yourself skills, whether food production or building construction (as Henry Thoreau recommended), or pre-adapting a skill or hobby that could contribute to a part-time income.

For example, consider Jeff, a local acquaintance who helped me out recently. In his personal "moon-lighting" job, Jeff recently fixed my car's chipped windshield. He told me that if he ever loses his shoe sales job in a nearby city, he could relatively easily expand his windshield repair business while waiting to be rehired or until something new came along. Also, in a surprising reversal of trends, the U.S.D.A. recently reported that more and more young couples are getting involved in farming, especially in the production of small scale, organic, specialty crops.

Another example: years ago The Wall St. Journal had an article entitled "On Their Own" exploring how a number of International Harvester workers in Ft. Wayne, Indiana, had set up their own small, part-time business. What is perhaps so unusual about this situation is that, unlike most large corporations, International Harvester apparently did not frown on its employees moonlighting. In fact, one time when an employee complained to his supervisor that he wasn't getting sufficient satisfaction from his job, his boss (as an example of Facilitator-As-Gardener) responded by encouraging him to "get something more interesting going on the side." And judging from the interviews, that's precisely what many of the workers did.

Take, for example, Stan Urbine. When not drafting or designing Harvester parts, Stan and his brother, Greg, were designing and manufacturing specialty parts for race cars. Then there was Daryl Banet who enjoys repairing cars and tractors in his backyard garage. Also mentioned were part-time carpenters, upholsterers, salespersons, and semiprofessional photographers. These "moonlighting entrepreneurs" not only made extra income from their self-directed, part-time business, but also made their lives more interesting while engaging in outside activities. Equally important, their secondary jobs (like Ware's description of the Lynn shoemakers of a hundred and fifty years ago) gave these workers something to fall back on when faced with the inevitable layoff due to restructurings, outsourcing, or the eventual business-cycle recession. Indeed, Harvester did finally close its truck facility less than two years later after the article was written.[3]

Although not necessarily a perfect solution to the high levels of unemployment of the Great Depression of the 1930's or the more recent Great Recession, who can fail to see that such arrangements make for a sense of some empowerment or psychic security among affected workers? And when the inevitable layoffs finally arrive, chances are that there will be no black despair, no thoughts of suicide among the Stan Urbines or Daryl Banets of the working world!

This is indeed an interesting model to consider. Recently there have been discussions about Germany's system of life-time manufacturing employment security (*Kurzarbeit*), a plan which is made possible by generous government subsidies during recessionary periods. It could be argued, however, that the German model is not so easily applicable in the U.S. given our culture, values, and proclivity for individualism and self-reliance.

This other arrangement—where the worker has the opportunity to seek out his or her small-scale entrepreneurial niche within the local economy—may be more realistic and more in tune with our nation's temperament and historic traditions.

PART II

Learning for All Ages

CHAPTER 7

Topsoil Drama

"The care of the earth is our most ancient and most worthy and, after all, our most pleasing responsibility. To cherish what remains of it, and to foster its renewal, is our only legitimate hope."
—Wendell Berry

Topsoil, we know, makes human life possible on this planet. Yet how many of us realize that creating topsoil is a slow, slow process and losing it can be dishearteningly swift? Surely these are important facts for all of us to learn, and especially important to impress upon young people.

With this thought in mind, I felt that a natural history of soils might be a useful, even fun topic when my wife asked me to do a project for her Girl Scout Day Camp. Starting with a suggestion from Del Thomas, a local soil scientist, we decided to create a "Topsoil Drama." In addition, we tried to make our little play relatively simple so that others might try it with minimal cost and preparation. Here then is an account of what we did:

We first gathered some twenty girls, aged seven to twelve, for a one-hour activity. Beginning with the suggestion that they pick up some soil and ask themselves: "How important is this in keeping us all alive?" The question created an opportunity for everyone to think about the essential nature of what we often refer to in (a negative way) as "dirt." Of course, all our vegetables, our fruit, and our grains are directly dependent upon topsoil, and most everything else we eat is indirectly dependent upon it as well.

“What about pizza? How do the ingredients, including meat and cheese directly or indirectly depend upon topsoil? What about lumber for our homes, paper for books and writing, cotton and wool to keep up warm? What about butterflies and bumblebees, foxes and meadowlarks?” Yes, virtually all land-dwelling animals depend upon a food chain that begins with the miracle of water, sunlight, seeds, combined with this dark crumbly substance that’s ever-present beneath our feet.

Next question: “Where does our soil come from?” Here I brought out a jar of water with a tablespoon of alum mixed in. (The alum, which can be purchased at a grocery store, helps separate the various soil components.)

We then put a handful of our collected soil into the water, screwed the lid tight and let everyone give the jar a shake. Within a minute it became obvious that the soil had at least three components: first, the small stones and sand that lay on the bottom, next, the fine clay particles in the middle, and finally, the decomposed vegetable matter floating on top. After observing this, I asked the girls if they would like to be in a play in which we could “make” some topsoil.

“Yes!” they shouted.

“OK, let’s begin at the beginning—that is, with rock from an ancient mountain or volcano, which over time, is broken up by the steady erosion of wind and water. Which of you wants to be a *volcano*?” Many hands shot up.

I chose a volunteer and placed a prepared *volcano* sign around her neck. From our son’s rock collection, I had brought a sample of volcanic rock in the form of a hand-sized piece of lightweight pumice. We passed it around and then gave it back to the person designated *volcano*.

“Anyone want to be *water*?” We got a couple of volunteers and gave them *water* signs. “Now who wants to be *wind*?”

I explained that *wind* and *water* will act on these rocks as they did over billions of years, to break up the large boulders into smaller pieces of stone and eventually into sand. I also pointed out that these sand particles were moved about by water and eventually come to rest. There they sat. And with more and more sand coming in, compressing the bottom layers to the point where they were literally cemented together. This newer, compressed rock is called “bedrock sandstone.” (In our area, we have many outcroppings of Cambrian sandstones dating back about five-hundred million years.)

I pulled out a piece of local sandstone and asked, "Who wants to play the part of *bedrock*?" I chose half a dozen *bedrocks*, put signs on them and asked the girls to huddle together on the ground. Now when we start our Topsoil Drama, *wind* and *water* will "wave" and "blow" through the *bedrocks*, breaking the rock back into individual sand particles.

Next, we needed someone to become *glacier*. (Here in the Midwest, glaciers came through at various times in the past two million years, ripping up bedrock, grinding the pieces down, and carrying the soil-making material to our area. Some of the sand in our jar probably came from hundreds of miles north of us.) *Glacier*, in our drama, had the job of crunching and grinding and moving rock and sand across the landscape.

The rest of the girls, except one, were given signs representing small to microscopic *animals* (including moles, worms, mites, insect larvae, nematodes, and, of course, bacteria) while others would be *plants*. As *plants*, the girls would fall on the ground, wriggle up, fall down and wriggle up, again and again in imitation of the year-to-year cycle of plants growing, dying, and growing up again and again.

At this point, we briefly returned to the jar of water and soil. We noted that the girls acting as *plants* would eventually "become" the floating humus (decayed matter) floating on top of the water, while the finer particles would be in the middle, and the broken up bedrock would end up as sand at the bottom of the jar.

Finally, the one remaining girl played *mother time*. Her job was to hold up her hands and hover over the topsoil drama activity.

We could now begin the play. And what a scene it was! *Volcano's* pumice was thrown up again and again. *Wind* and *water* broke up the *bedrocks* while *glacier* came through moving the *bedrocks* even more. Meanwhile, *plants* grew up, died, grew up and died again, at a steady pace as *animals* also did their important work. After a few minutes, I asked the girls to stop everything while taking a moment to appreciate how much time it took to "make" soil.

"Once bedrock is broken up, it takes approximately five-hundred years to make one inch of topsoil!"

"Let's now pretend that every ten seconds is a hundred years of time. Everyone freeze and consider all the things that are happening. *Mother time* will hold her hands over the scene, and we will call out every one hundred years (every ten seconds). Remember, nobody can move."

"One hundred years…two hundred years…three hundred years…"

Frozen kids.

Each ten seconds seemed unbearably long. "Four hundred years…and finally five hundred years."

"And after all this work, this is what we have." I pulled a towel off a pie pan and on the bottom was one inch of soil. It was a grand achievement!

"But," I asked, "Is it enough to grow a tree?"

"No."

"Could it grow corn?"

"No."

A small seedling, at best, might grow in this one inch of soil. We would obviously have to make much more if we ever wanted to grow a tree.

While we were discussing this last point, a gust of wind came through, creating an opportunity to demonstrate wind erosion. Picking up some soil from the pan, I let it blow out of my hands. Another handful, and suddenly most of the soil was gone.

I was beginning to sense an element of frustration, even anger. All that work! All that time put into making our little inch of soil, and now it was so easily, so quickly lost to a few gusts of wind. We looked down at the pan. It was a depressing sight—a little bit of soil but mostly spots of bare, polished aluminum. Now we couldn't even grow a seedling.

We then walked over to a worn path that went down a bank to a nearby creek. The path was bare of vegetation and had begun to show signs of erosion.

"Why is the path losing its soil?"

We noted that the vegetation, which contributes to the making of soil, is also important in keeping the soil from washing away, especially on steep slope. I then put the last of our topsoil on the path and asked the girls where they thought it would eventually end up.

It was obvious that the next rain would carry this loose soil down to the stream below. We mentally followed its inevitable trip to the west into our local Red Cedar River, then into the Chippewa River, the Mississippi and finally into the Gulf of Mexico. (Here it would be helpful to have a large map of the U.S.) Then, with all of us standing still, I once again asked them to remain quiet for a moment and think about what we had learned.

The long geological and biological processes of soil-building plus the depressing feeling of losing it to erosion; these were the things I wanted the girls not only to know and especially to feel.

Hopefully then, from our Topsoil Drama experience, these girls will be more understanding, more respectful, indeed more vigilant in preserving the wonderful topsoil we still have—a resource so amazing, so precious, and as we witnessed this day, so very vulnerable too.

CHAPTER 8

A Passion to Learn

"Years ago, I wrote that many people in their worst nightmares find themselves once again a student in school... Many mature and competent adults tell me that to this day they feel uneasy in a school building, as if they were guilty of some crime, but didn't know what."
—John Holt

I wonder: is it possible to teach ecological values or nurture an ecological consciousness? Of course some teachers make an effort to encourage students to know about geology and geography as well as understanding the relationships of plants and animals, woodlands and wetlands, soils and microorganisms. Others may teach about global warming, green energy, environmentally friendly cities as well as sustainable development and low-carbon transportation systems. Yet I wonder if teachers should aim for something more, something beyond knowledge itself. What would that goal be?

In my view, the object of teaching is to somehow instill a *passion to learn*. If teachers are doing their job, they will help their students acquire a lifetime love of learning. If those students happen to be interested in ecology, that passion then becomes the fuel to launch them both outward and inward into deepening their knowledge, insights, and understandings.

The objective is thus not the result of short-term scores on standardized knowledge tests, but the student's long-run delight in continuous learning—until the end of their lives. If teachers don't somehow move their students toward this goal, even in a small way, I don't think they can be considered completely successful.

Deep down I have the feeling that nurturing a passion for learning should not be difficult. The process of growing and becoming a more self-reliant learner, of prospecting for humankind's great creations and discoveries ought to be an exciting adventure full of delights and surprises that touch both heart and mind.

Yet as we know, this is often not the case. Teachers with enthusiasm and the best of intentions frequently end up as mechanical dispensers of information and facts. Many feel that the only way they can overcome students' resistance to learning is to force-feed them by methods of power and fear.

Power and fear! These are all too often the tools used to get the job done. What a frustrating environment this must be for a new teacher with high hopes and good intentions. And from the viewpoint of the students who recall the fun of learning new things on their own before schooling and who wish to become persons of greater value during their lifetime, the situation's even worse. Such students must feel robbed. What was once an inner-directed drive for learning is now based upon pleasing the teacher or worse, to pass mandated tests so one can successfully "get through the system." For those who eventually want to become self-learners, undoing the damage is difficult if not impossible—like trying to decontaminate radioactive substances.

Is there any hope for this state of affairs? Unfortunately it appears less and less likely particularly with the trend toward online courses, where a student may not even encounter a living teacher as role model.

Yet given a traditional (live teacher) classroom environment, there are examples in which these suffocating outcomes do not occur. Indeed, among the various teachers I have known, a few have been able to avoid the pitfalls. These teachers did not succumb to the usual mechanical teaching. Instead, they retained their enthusiasm year after year, and what is even more amazing, they succeeded in nurturing a genuine excitement for learning. What was their secret? What qualities did these memorable teachers have in common? From my observations, each of these teachers possessed three characteristics.

First, they all put a high priority on creating a positive attitude toward their subject matter, as opposed to the usual goal of simply imparting a certain body of knowledge. It's not that knowledge and facts were unimportant, but the subject matter should be used as a vehicle to get students excited about the process of learning. Teachers can tell if they are on the right track by listening to their students: such comments as "boy, do I love history," or "I think I will audit a literature class next semester" is a good indicator that self-learning is not far off.

The second quality is for the teacher to knit together other areas of knowledge into the class while incorporating the students' own experiences and current level of knowledge. This quality implied that the teacher herself is interested in diverse subjects and thus also becomes a good role-model for self-learning.

I believe students often feel certain disconnectedness as they travel from one box of knowledge to another. The sum often becomes less than the disconnected parts. Unfortunately students rarely develop the skills that will help them tie these seemingly disconnected parts together. But when a holistic integration is done expertly such as with a Carl Sagan, a Loren Eiseley, a Lewis Thomas or a Ken Burns, the performance can be breathtaking. Yet there seems to be little or no attempt in our schools, from kindergarten to graduate school, to cultivate the integrative skills or reward teachers who pursue them. Perhaps it is collegial pressures or simply ingrained teaching habits that make it so difficult for teachers to climb over the high walls of discipline specialization as we pursue our day-to-day classroom encounters with our students.

But now let us assume that we can avoid the problems cited above. Also assume that we are able to retain our enthusiasm—and yet, we still find our students unhappy and resentful. It's a situation, in which things ought to be okay, but instead we find resistance; we simply have not awakened in our students their innate potential for learning. What's wrong? What have we missed?

This brings us to the third and perhaps most difficult quality, for it involves some decontamination on the part of the teachers themselves. The third quality that outstanding teachers have is a high regard for the student. Actually it's more than that. These teachers consistently demonstrate a profound respect for the students' native intelligence and potential for discovery and insight.

This means, for example, that teachers of physics would give the same respect, the same esteem to each student that they would give to the great geniuses of the discipline; for example to a young Marie Curie or Albert Einstein if they were sitting in the classroom.

For many teachers, this third quality involves a radical rethinking of what education is all about. Indeed, we find no simple techniques that will help teachers out on this one. But when the respect is there, it's there. The students know it. Respect is transmitted in a thousand little ways, operating like a magic whirlpool that loosens up tight muscles of resistance and thaws out cold fear.

When teachers genuinely respect their students, the relationship is no longer one based on power and fear, but on equality. When a student says something impressive, the teacher is truly impressed and, indeed, might gain new insights or perspectives on the issues or topic at hand. The essential source of authority teachers have is simply some extra knowledge in an interesting or useful discipline—nothing more. Traditional authority and power have no place in the relationship.

In the end, respect brings respect, resulting in a situation in which students may become truly engaged learners, often in surprising ways. Those few successful teachers know the truth of this. How did they learn it? I don't know, perhaps by trial and error, perhaps by instinct.

However, I do know that teachers who combine these three qualities—a positive attitude, integrated presentations, and a consistent and deep respect for their students—will, in their own small way, move them closer to becoming self-reliant learners. The students may then begin to deepen their understanding, to evolve authentic personal philosophies and values while gaining sufficient confidence to adapt to life's ever-changing challenges, all fruits of a life-time passion to learn.

CHAPTER 9

High-Jumping

"Of all the formulations of play,
the briefest and best is to be found in Plato's Law's.
He sees the model of true playfulness
in the need of all creatures, animal and human, to leap. To
truly leap you must learn how to use the ground
as a springboard, and how to land resiliently and safely.
It means to test the leeway allowed by given limits;
to outdo and yet not escape gravity."
—Erik Erickson

"I am thankful for my body.
It lets me jump, run and walk. I like it."
—Cayden Cooper

Healthy lives strive for healthy bodies as well as healthy learning environments. Indeed, doesn't the animal within whisper to us to get up and get away from the dull glare of our electronic screens, to flee from our seat-bound offices and commuter confinements, to move and delight (like other animals) in multifarious motions, activities, and sundry skills?

Consider the urge to run or simply saunter about, to launch or hit a ball, to dance away the night, to execute a karate smack, or climb rocks, or glide into T'ai chi's "Wave Hands Like Clouds"—or simply to leap, to spring up and test your body's many powers!

I'm assuming that most readers have a favorite physical activity and, along with it, a personal story to share. For me, I feel lucky that my athletic urge connects me with my family culture and early education. It's a story that begins over a hundred years ago in the little village of Blue Mound, Illinois. In our family photo collection there is a picture of my grandfather (as a young boy) high jumping in the backyard of his Blue Mound home. I treasure this photograph for it connects him with me. You see, I love to high jump too.

In fact jumping has been a minor passion of mine from grade school right into middle age. Just about everywhere I've lived, I constructed a set of crude high-jump standards and found a suitable crossbar. That's pretty much all one needs—except, of course, a soft place to land.

I need to confess right off that, despite my obsession with jumping, I'm not a very good high jumper. High schoolers today who jump only as high as I do would not make the track and field team. Many years ago, our young son asked me quite honestly if I "was approaching the world's record." (He liked to be proud of his dad, if for no other reason than to brag to his friends.) He soon learned the truth as verified by his own copy of *The Guinness Book of World Records*; that his father jumps more than four feet below what the best jumpers do today. Not very impressive. If my memory is correct, I actually jumped higher in the ninth or tenth grade; but even then, I never made the team.

I'm often haunted by the thought that if I had made the team or had been forced to jump in a physical education class, I'd probably now have little, if any, interest in high jumping. I am intrigued, for example, by the late George Sheehan's question: "What happened to our play on our way to becoming adults?" His answer

"*Downgraded by the intellectuals, dismissed by the economists, put aside by the psychologists, it was left to the teachers to deliver the coup de grace. Physical education was born and turned what was joy into boredom, what was fun into drudgery, what was pleasure into work.*"[1]

One might speculate what other amateur enjoyment and later-life pleasures were also diminished or even ruined by a coercive environment of conventional schooling.

Thus it is not for achievement, honor, or record heights that I jump. I jump simply because I enjoy it. First, I enjoy thinking about the jump beforehand, then the translation of thought into action—slowly running toward the bar, speeding up on the last step or two, and then in a flash, hurtling myself over.

Sometime I experiment with different speeds, different steps and different zones of concentration. Like any other sport, high jumping can be infinitely complicated or wonderfully simple. The pure analytical side is interesting; but more exciting is the sense of abandon, of letting go. I have, however, yet to feel anything grandiose. For me, there's been no mystical Zen satori, no ecstasies to report back. Yet I can honestly say that there have been rare instances that I've actually felt like I was, well, *flying*, if only for an instant. It was not unlike that wonderfully sensation which I once, when very young, felt in dreams. I have also been able to jump without thinking of anything in particular—just feeling fully connected to my surroundings and to the present moment: feet against dirt, wind and sun on my back, listening to the intermittent sounds of crows and crickets (great jumpers themselves!), and in the distance, the call of a mourning dove. All the while I am loping toward the bar when suddenly I spring up—converting horizontal momentum into vertical flight.

To jump any reasonable height takes balance, rhythm, coordination, and good form. My jumping style is the old-fashioned Western Roll, first perfected by Stanford high-jumper George Horne in 1912. It is a technique that takes more time to learn than the easy Scissors or the simple Straddle (jumping as if you had tried to leap into a horse's back and wound up on the other side), or even today's universally popular "Fosbury Flop."

In jumping the Western Roll, I take off from my inside foot while kicking my outside foot as hard and as high as I can. As my kicking leg approaches the bar, my body and takeoff leg quickly rise to join the upper leg so that everything "rolls" over pretty much at the same time. A photograph taken at the instant of clearance shows the jumper as if lying on his side, parallel to the cross-bar, with the kicking leg stretched out and his takeoff leg slightly tucked in near the bar. Unlike some of the other jumping styles, such as the Scissors, Straddle or Fosbury Flop, here everything goes over the bar simultaneously, thus enhancing the sensation of "flying."

I was surprised to learn that no recent athlete has broken the world's high-jump record using this technique. But in 1912, George Horne cleared six feet, seven inches (a record for his era), and more recently, Gene Johnson cleared a little over seven feet using a Western Roll technique. However today's best jumpers, using the Fosbury Flop, are currently leaping some eight feet in height.

Let me repeat that I jump because I like to jump. I've jumped in the rain, and I've jumped when there was snow on the ground. Sometimes I will jump when I don't feel very well. Often I've discovered that the way I jump tells me something about my physical or mental state.

I've also discovered that high jumping can be an interesting exercise in learning to confront fear. Anytime you jump at chest level or above, you're taking some physical risk. There the metal bar sits—unwavering, inelastic, and uncompromisingly hard. The bar I use is triangular, made of an aluminum alloy, and has sharp edges. If my knee hits it, it can be quite painful. I've also sprained my jumping foot, and it is not unusual for me to hurt my back or wrist.

A good jump puts you relatively high into the air and, sooner or later, you must return to the earth. Yet I have discovered that it is nearly impossible to make a satisfying jump when I have even the slightest air of caution in my approach. At the moment of take off, one must simply surrender to an instantaneous intuition. A good jump, in short, involves an element of faith that everything will go successfully. Yet as often happens, a speck of fear intrudes at the last moment, forcing me either to abort or make a miserable and often painful jump. (Could this, I wonder, be a metaphor for other adventures in life?)

So perhaps now you understand why I've enjoyed jumping over the years. It's somehow wrapped up in the thrill of animal power, the skill of form, the lighthearted sense of letting go, and sometimes the feeling of flight. Perhaps someday it might be even more than that.

Why couldn't high jumping (or any similar sport) evolve into a more mystical state such as can be found in the martial arts of Asia? Why couldn't we experience, after sufficient skill development and concentration, something equivalent to what archer Eugen Herrigel describes in his book *Zen in the Art of Archery* as a state of "serene pulsation which can be heightened into the feeling, otherwise experienced only in rare dreams, of extraordinary lightness, and in the rapturous certainly of being able to summon up energies in any direction."[2] It's surely something to look forward to.

But in the meantime, for me at least, I'll continue my unspectacular leaps. With friendly crickets nearby or thoughts of childhood and my Grandpa Bauer jumping in Blue Mound Illinois; with corn rustling in the garden, prairie grasses bending in the wind, the sun disappearing behind a cloud, I'm off!

PART III

On Evolution

CHAPTER 10

Celebrating our Cosmic Journey

"Why should I feel lonely? Is not our planet in the Milky Way?"
—Henry Thoreau

Who hasn't felt a shiver down their spine contemplating the vastness of the cosmos? Or asked themselves: "How did it begin?" or "Exactly where do we fit within the ongoing evolution of the Universe?" More often than not, these questions are rekindled in thoughts and conversations as we step out under the bright stars of a dark night. Indeed, I recall so well that mild summer evening years ago when our nine-year old daughter and I walked hand in hand to the back of our property. On that unusually dark and beautiful night, we made our way to a secluded part of our land. Earlier, I had set up a small telescope in a relatively flat, unobstructed viewing area. We then pointed the telescope toward the lovely constellation of Lyra, the "Harp" configuration of stars between the constellations of Cygnus and Hercules.

Next, we took a peek at Lyra's unusual Ring Nebula, a donut-like gray-green wisp of fluorescence— or as some might say: "a faint puff of smoke from some far-off pipe." What we saw was actually a dying star some twenty-three hundred light-years away. Astronomers tell us that Lyra's ring is actually a bubble of hot gas expanding ever outward—a gentle but final "shrug" of a relatively small star that was once much like our own sun. We were, in a sense, witnessing a grand preview of our own stellar future.

Of course, our sun's solar swelling and superheated ring-puff will happen over a billion years from now—plenty of time for good digestion, a long, long life, plus sufficient geological time for millions of future generations of Earth-bound species, including ourselves. But eventually our home star will also change into what astronomers call a "Red Giant." It will swell and burn with intensity. Its expanding heat and searing bubble will burn Earth's precious skin of green and atmospheric blue. It will vaporize rivers and oceans alike, boil away every stream and splash of puddle.

"But" my daughter asked, "Will people be able to live? Would we need to wear space suits? Could we move to Pluto?"

I was impressed with her strategies for survival. Of course, it may be possible to extend life elsewhere. But eventually our Sun's inevitable burnout will leave scant hope for life-forms within this planetary neighborhood. In the meantime, what should we do?

Perhaps we should simply share the beauty, share the evening's friendship and wonder while witnessing the moment, this moment in the here and the now. That night my daughter and I chatted about our feelings and life's meaning. We, mixed into our hour some science and silence while experiencing the deepening darkness and relishing the night's enchantment. Also that August evening, we saw some meteors. My companion counted eleven. Excitedly she nudged me—"Look, look!!"

As we packed up our telescope, we made a date to go out again. But next time we would observe not star destruction, but stellar creation. We promised each other that come winter, we would take a peek at Orion's bright nebula, a zone of the night sky that astronomers have described as a "stellar nursery." In observing Orion's luminous dust "cloud," one can actually witness infant stars in the making, baby stars sparkling through the blue-green glow of Orion's galactic mist. Such are some of the ongoing destructions and creations of our ever-evolving universe.

My daughter and I would both make one last glance overhead, taking in the unearthly stillness while admiring the dark and deepening beauty. Again, who has not sensed large questions coming on while standing so small under the sweep of stars and the mystery of the night?

If I could, I would like to find out where we came from, to follow back that old trail of universal time and visit some of the landmarks of our cosmic history. In order to make familiar the evolutionary sequences that brought us to this moment of consciousness, then to invite these cosmic events into the mind and heart, not with fearful strangeness, but with understanding and affection—like writer C.S. Lewis once described the familiar as "soft slippers, old cloths, old jokes and the thump of a sleepy dog's tail on the kitchen floor."[1]

What happened then, in the interval from that original emptiness to this moment that I sit at my desk tapping the keys of an old Royal typewriter while enjoying the distant trill of a resident field sparrow?

Both modern science and many mythological creation stories believe that in the beginning, there was a pause. It might help to try and imagine pure space, pure emptiness. It's interesting to note that there are large zones of the night sky where there's practically nothing: "Cosmic Voids" they are called. Two voids that have been closely studied are the Bootes Void (named after the constellation that depicts a mythological herder) and the one in Coma Bernice's (The Hair of Bernice). You might try to find these constellations on some dark night in the spring. Then relax, take your time and imagine the great gaps within. Can you somehow sense the great emptiness just before the universe began?

To get into the mood, I sometimes look through the telescope at an empty area of the night sky, away from the great masses of stars. For me, at least, this is the starting point. I look and look and look, taking in the magnified circle of magnificent blackness. On these special nights I will often bring to mind a quotation from the Chinese *Tao Te Ching*, the great spiritual poem of Taoism:

"The Way is a void/ Used but never filled / An abyss it is / Like an ancestor/ From which all things come.../ Whose offspring it may be / I do not know / It is like a preface to God."[2]

Again, I put my eye to the eyepiece and look into the empty space. Within the ring of blackness, I sense a perfect quiet from some mysterious, creative Source:

"There is a being, wonderful, perfect / It existed before heaven and earth. How quiet it is! How spiritual it is! / It stands alone and does not change. It moves around and around but does not on this account suffer. All life comes from it. / It wraps everything with its love as in a garment...I do not know its name."[3]

Consider too the many Native American creation stories, some of them surprisingly similar to the above description of the origins of the cosmos. One of my favorite legends involves an Original Being called Maheo whose mood, it was said, could determine the state of the universe:

"At first there was nothing. In the beginning there was nothing in all of time and space. Only was there darkness and Maheo. If Maheo was silent, then the Universe was still...All around Maheo was nothingness and silence, age upon age."[4]

Then Maheo began to realize the power he had could be translated into the power to create! From that insight, he reasoned that "Power is nothing until it has been used to do something." Armed with both power and insight, Maheo concluded that it was time to act:

"He took all of time, past and present and future, and gathered it in one hand. Into his other hand he gathered all space. With these in each hand he clapped. A great clap it was, greater than thunder. For this clap was the first sound every heard in the Universe."[5]

Continuing the story, we learn that from this first clap:

" ...came all things, and everything from which all things could be made...Stars came flying out of his hands like sparks from crackling wood in a fire. Everywhere did the stars fly out and continue to fly out and burn today everywhere across the night-time sky. This is how time began and all things began to be made."[6]

To a modern astronomer, Maheo's initial "Clap of Creation" is surprisingly similar to the Big Bang theory of the beginnings of the universe (with the addition of some universally familiar audio/ visual effects: "…like sparks from crackling wood in a fire").

Consider too the Old Testament's creation story of Genesis 1:3. The biblical description brings to light an important detail that conforms nicely to recent scientific theory. Recall that on the first day of creation, before Earth had formed, "God said, Let there be light: and there was light." Physicist Chet Raymo, author of numerous books on astronomy, thinks that the Big Bang was actually misnamed. Instead of The Big Bang, he suggests calling it the "The Big Flash," an event of some 13.8 billion years ago consisting of "an infinitely dense and infinitely hot seed of energy"[7] coming essentially out of nothingness. And as the universe fed upon its elementary diet of light and gravity waves, the primeval cosmos literally flowed from physical matter into light and back into matter. Of that stupendous, creative moment, cosmologist Gary Bennett writes:

"Packet of energy called photons raced through the early universe...In a sense the universe at this state was light...Although the temperature had cooled a lot since the since the inception of the universe less than a millionth of a second before, it was still enormously hot—hundreds of time hotter than a detonating hydrogen bomb. At these temperatures, matter emerged as elementary particles when photon collided with photon. Einstein's famous equation E = mc2 beautifully documents this early era when energy and matter flowed back and forth interchangeably."[8]

And so what happened after this grand opening event of our universe? Professor Raymo states that, (I detect here almost a yawn as if the hard part was essentially over): "the universe was off and running."

After a millisecond of extreme expansion, (the "era of inflation"), astronomers mark an event—about four minutes after the Big Bang—where the universe "cooled" down to approximately a billion degrees. At this point, its elemental composition consisted of some 75 percent hydrogen and 25 percent helium. Virtually all the heavier elements such as carbon and oxygen would thereafter be manufactured in the process of star births and star deaths, that is in the interiors of planetary nebulae (such as Lyra's Ring Nebula), and even more importantly, within the titanic explosions of supernovas, intense zones of radical destructions and fused creations, of atoms compressed into heavier and heavier elements: hydrogen fusing into helium and on to carbon, oxygen, silicon, and iron, ever recycling, ever evolving.

So where do we look? In what direction of the night sky did the Big Bang event take place? In actuality, we are of the Big Bang and are currently coevolving with it after nearly fourteen billion years. In response to the question: "Where did it take place? We learn that the Big Bang "occurred everywhere... space itself came into existence with the Big Bang."[9] Indeed, the remnants of the event can still be "heard" today via microwave radiation that "hums" smoothly and evenly from each and every part of the sky. Unable to pinpoint a single direction, I confess to some disappointment, as if I had run into an invisible barrier in investigating a crucial detail of my "family" history.

However, the next stage of cosmic evolution offers greater possibilities for getting a feeling for, and a connection to our early universe. Gary Bennett continues his description of the early moments:

"As hydrogen and helium spewed forth from the primeval fireball, instabilities in the material formed and grew. Vast clouds of hydrogen and helium, each billions of times more massive than the Sun, fell together under the pull of gravity to make protogalaxies. Inside the newborn galaxies, turbulent regions of gas coalesced under gravity into stars.[10]

Indeed, we can detect these very young, massive galaxies through their radiation sources called "quasars." Quasars appear to be fantastic powerhouses, stupendous beacons of radiation; the oldest of them date back to just 800 million years after the Big Bang. This makes the telescopes which detect them equivalent to scientific time machines, witnessing the universe as it existed when it was only about 5% of its current age.

Quasars or "quasi-stellar radio sources" were thus formed within the interiors of ancient galaxies. These galactic cores, in turn, contained super massive black holes that actively "fed" on gas (and sometimes stars) in that early cosmic era. A black hole's intense gravity can so distort the fabric of space; it is able to "capture" light waves passing too close to the intense gravitational field. Yet just before the final descent of matter into the blackness of no return, some ultra hot elements (heated by friction) beam out as powerful quasar flares, sending pulses of radiation billions of light years across the universe.

Astronomers may disagree about some of the details of the Big Bang and its immediate aftermath, but there is little argument over what you and I can see when we step out on a clear, moonless night. Nearby, in time and space, we can witness friendly stars, beautiful stars and, of course, many of the age-old constellations that are easily accessible with a pair of binoculars or simply a slight bend of the neck. And those lucky enough to experience a clear night sky—without light pollution—can also enjoy that lovely river of light we call the Milky Way.

In his book, *Armchair Astronomy*, British author Patrick Moore explains that it would be theoretically possible for a single star to escape from a galaxy such as the Milky Way:

"Once beyond the galactic halo, a star would be beyond the limit of detection...particularly if it were a star no more luminous that the sun. We can visualize the sky as seen from a planet moving round such a star. The night sky would be virtually blank; nothing would be seen apart from dim glows in

the extreme distance. It would seem decidedly lonely, and I think we must be grateful that our Sun is is not a solitary wanderer in space between the galaxies."[11]

But as we know, we do have an intimate galactic neighborhood, a cosmic home, visible as a lovely, creamy-white trail of countless specks of light above our heads on a dark, clear night. In the Milky Way, there are some two hundred billion stars in addition to our own Sun. And not only can we easily see an intensely star-dense segment of our galaxy, but we also know something about the galaxy's overall size, its rotation, and its general appearance. In addition, we are lucky to live in an age when astronomers can, with reasonable accuracy, pinpoint our planet's position within the Milky Way's vast, wheel-like superstructure.

To bring the Milky Way into perspective, on a very small scale mind you, one might begin with a cup of hot water and a spoonful of instant coffee. Once you submerge the crystals, give the liquid a clockwise spin. Within seconds, you have created a miniature galaxy out of the swirling bubbles. A coffee galaxy will usually consist of a central core of densely packed bubbles and two or three well-defined spiral arms spinning around and around against a backdrop of inky blackness.

Assuming you make one of these coffee galaxies, you have now re-created a surprisingly good representation of our Milky Way. Your coffee galaxy is perhaps two or three inches across; the Milky Way, in contrast, is some 120 thousand light-years from edge to edge. (Recall that a light-year is the distance that light can travel in a year's time—approximately six trillion miles.) In comparison, the closest galaxy similar in size to the Milky Way—the Andromeda Galaxy—is about two and one-half million light-years away.

As we visualize the Milky Way slowly swirling through space, we might also begin asking additional questions. For example, "Where does the Earth reside in respect to the galaxy's central region and its flowing arms?

Telescopic data indicate that our sun's location is neither in the center nor on the edge of the Milky Way. Our galactic arm fragment or "spur" (the Orion Spur) is between the inner Sagittarius Arm and the outermost Perseus Arm. Residing within the Orion Spur, our sun is some twenty-six thousand light-years from the galactic center or just a little less than half-way from the Milky Way's nucleus to its outer edge.

Perhaps on some cold winter's evening, you will find yourself taken in by the Milky Ways' great river of stars coursing across the sky. If so, try to find the beautiful Pleiades, (Seven Sisters) in the constellation Taurus (not far from the more famous Orion Constellation). If you can find the Pleiades, your line of sight will be looking essentially in the opposite direction from the galactic center.

In late summer, however, you will have another opportunity to reorient yourself, only now your line of sight will be directed toward the interior zones of our galaxy. For example, when you look at the constellation Cygnus (the Swan), you will be looking toward the inner part of the Orion Spur, toward the stellar roadway which would lead you round the spiral system toward the center of the galaxy. Our solar system is, in fact, moving in Cygnus' direction as we circle the Milky Way's nucleus.

Now look toward the constellation Sagittarius (the Archer) which is best seen from a lawn chair on a clear, moonless night in August. (North American observers can follow the Milky Way's starry river down to the southern horizon.) As you look toward the southern horizon you may not see a well-defined archer, but an arrangement of stars that resembles a teapot.

Now if you could shoot a cosmic arrow toward the spout of that teapot, your arrow would travel through trillions of miles of space—through dark, obscuring dust clouds and massive star clusters, and finally some twenty-six thousand light-years away, your arrow would penetrate the heart of the Milky Way's nucleus. Because of intervening dust and gas, the Milky Way's central core is all but invisible—even to the most powerful optical telescopes. Yet it can be "seen" with instruments that are capable of measuring infrared, X-ray, ultraviolet, and other forms of high-level energies. Thus, on an imaginary journey to the Milky Way's center, we would eventually come upon (as Professor Raymo describes it):

"a monstrous pulsing heart of the galaxy, a core of violence that recapitulates the violence of the creation itself. The nucleus of the Milky Way Galaxy is apparently the site for cosmic convulsions on the grand scale, perhaps a place where countless suns are swallowed up by a massive gravitational black hole."[12]

We can now begin to experience that all-important "sense of place" not just our local landscape or even in a planetary context, but also on a galactic scale. As we have seen, of greatest importance is the fact that we reside at a relatively safe distance, "in the suburbs," so to speak, far away from the lethal pulses of radiation from the central core.

But wouldn't it be interesting if there was some way to get a photograph or at least construct an image of what our galaxy might look like from a distance, to somehow capture the Milky Way's elegant form and inherent beauty in its entirety? Given the hundred and twenty thousand light-year span of the Milky Way, humans may never see our home galaxy from such a distant vantage point. Yet it is relatively easy to take a look at a close neighbor—the Great Galaxy of Andromeda—a spiral galaxy surprisingly similar to our own in both size and shape.

To locate Andromeda's fuzzy congregation of stars, it helps to have a constellation chart on hand as well as a pair of binoculars. If you want to increase your chances of success, try viewing it on a moonless night in mid-to late September, when mosquitoes have disappeared and darkness arrives relatively early. First, can you find the North Star via the Big Dipper? Next, find the constellation Cassiopeia, located on the other side of the North Star (from the Big Dipper). Cassiopeia's most conspicuous feature is a compact group of stars in the shape of a "W. " Note that the bottom of the "W" consists of two sharp "pointers" directing your line of sight in a southerly direction. Using the upper pointer, sweep your binoculars to the right until you come upon our sister galaxy's faint, fuzzy smudge. Congratulations! You just located the Great Andromeda Galaxy.

As you look through the binoculars, Andromeda may not be a very spectacular sight. However you can magnify Andromeda not just through your eyes, but also in your mind. Consider Andromeda's three hundred billion stars. How many planets might it have and what varieties of life and other creations and fascinations? Consider too that Andromeda's light has traveled some two and a half million years before reaching your eyes. And, of course, the light from our own Milky Way galaxy of two and half million years ago (from that era of the earliest humanlike creatures such as Homo habilis) is now reaching Andromeda in a similar way, as a soft galactic glow.

Again, enjoy Andromeda (take your time) and then step back to consider the billions of other galaxies that are at this very moment evolving throughout the universe, the "music of the spheres" in the form of cosmic themes and variations that began some 13.8 billion years ago with the Big Bang. Now return to the Milky Way (our Milky Way!) and home into our own Sun and its family of planets. Can you make out that lovely blue and white cloud-swirled world below?

I have often wondered what it would be like to be an astronaut, to see the Earth from such a vantage point in space, and be that lucky observer from high above. How would it feel? Perhaps Louise Young, in her book The Blue Planet said it as well as any, reflecting on the beauty, delicacy, and the very miracle of it all:

"In the photographs of the earth from space, the planet looks like a little thing that I might hold in the hollow of my hand. I can imagine it would feel warm to the touch, vibrant and sensitive... Beneath the mobile membrane of cloud and air are a storehouse of splendors and a wealth of detail. There are rainbows caught in waterfalls, and frost flowers etched in window panes and drops of dew scattered like jewels on meadow grass, and honey creepers singing in the jacaranda tree."[13]

And finally we return to Earth, to our own lovely landscapes and familiar neighborhoods and to the comfort of knowing, "we are home!"

CHAPTER 11

Darwin's Finches & Ford's Mustangs

"The lucky individual that finds a different seed, or nook, or niche, will fly up and out from beneath the Sysphean rock of competition. It will tend to flourish and so will its descendants—that is, those that inherit the lucky character that had set it a little apart."

—Jonathan Weiner

"Survival of the fittest!"

Consider the many times we have heard this expression applied to the business world. Other phrases from the Darwinian world-view include: "finding a niche in the marketplace," "the struggle for existence," or the "extinction of a company or of a product line." How easily the ideas and vocabulary of evolutionary biology flow into the world of economics and back again.

But how accurate is the analogy? Is Darwin's theory of evolution via natural selection a workable metaphor for a business in pursuit of profit-making by innovating and marketing variations of products and services to consumers?

In one important sense—the method of creating variations—the business and Darwinian worlds are quite different. Natural selection for Darwin implied random variations of the offspring of living organisms. In contrast, businesses develop products through artificial selection, that is, through conscious and deliberate decisions on the part of designers, engineers, market researchers, and their focus groups. Nature uses a "shot-gun" approach, "inefficiently" producing a large number of offspring where some of them—by chance—will have an advantageous physical or behavioral trait that improves the chances of future reproductive success. Their offspring, in turn, will carry on that favorable trait, helping subsequent generations to survive.

To see how this works in greater detail, I would recommend reading Jonathan Weiner's excellent book, *The Beak of the Finch.* In it, the author describes the long-term studies of various species of finches living on the Galapagos Islands off the coast of Ecuador. The Galapagos studies which took place well over a hundred years after Darwin's visit (1835), suggest that it is relatively small variations—say in the depth or length of a finch's beak—that can make the difference in the survival of an individual bird, especially during time of environmental stress. Favored birds, as Darwin predicted, not only survive but will be more likely to successfully reproduce and pass on their genes into the next generation.

If, for example, Darwinian dynamics were applied to an automobile company, that company would have to manufacture thousands of slightly different models each year, hoping that one or a few might survive in the competitive marketplace. Such a wasteful and expensive process would obviously be both economically inefficient and unprofitable. Business must condense their selection process by artificially preselecting good designs, then market-test them in advance using a sample of potential buyers.

Today's automakers utilize 3D computer-animated modeling techniques (from which one can actually take a virtual "test drive"[1]) to search for potentially marketable designs from millions of possibilities. Indeed, why manufacture (as nature does) inefficient variations when they can be winnowed down through intelligent designs and scientific market research techniques?

However, once the selection process has narrowed the possibilities, then a business/biological analogy becomes more accurate. For example, if a company's product becomes successful, it attracts sufficient "resources" (revenues and profits) to keep it "alive," thereby guaranteeing its "reproduction" (continued manufacture) until there's a change in the overall economic "environment" (consumer preferences, manufacturing costs, foreign and domestic competition, etc.)

These lessons were highlighted years ago in Ford's epic Edsel failure and its surprising Mustang success. The Edsel's development included virtually no market research in the testing of potential stylistic variations. Although Ford placed its Edsel into a potentially profitable niche (occupied at the time by GM's Olds, Pontiac, and Buick), it projected a poor front-end design; in addition, early models suffered from substandard mechanical quality. Edsel's developers made the unforgivable mistake of offering a new and relatively untested push-button gearshift mechanism that was not only costly to produce, but suffered from an unacceptable high failure rate—nearly 50 percent in the first three months of sales! One could have predicted that sooner or later, the "species" Fordus edselus would become "extinct."

In contrast, Ford's Mustang is still alive in the automobile marketplace, projecting its familiar morphology (general body shape) after having gone through various transitional forms up to and including the Mustang of today. Both Mustang's name and styling had the advantage of detailed market research starting with demographic studies that forecasted a bulge of relatively young car buyers (postwar baby boomers) poised to purchase their first car. A biologist might say that "a new and viable niche was emerging."

For Ford, improved quality control would also be a key consideration. According to my father, Robert Eggert Sr. (who was Ford Division Manager of Market Research during this period), the reliability factor would be decisive, not just for the sales of new Mustangs, but would be an advantage in the used car market—a key to maintaining consumer brand loyalty.

In addition, the well-known name—"Mustang"—was chosen through a carefully planned and deliberate selection process. In the spring of 1963 Ford tested some thirty-three names. Focus groups were then asked to rate each name by the criteria: "suitability as a name for the special car" and a more generalized "feeling for the name" while viewing a pre-production clay model of the car's design.

In reviewing the original focus group results, I learned that the least popular names were Carnelian, Calli, and Fangio. Lee Iacocca, the vice president of the Ford Division pushed for Turino, a name that scored slightly below average in both criteria. The name Thunderbird II did better but not as well as Panther, Dolphin, or Commando. Mustang, a name inspired by the title of J. Frank Dobie's book *The Mustangs* scored the highest.

Next, how did the Mustang, in contrast to the Edsel, keep quality up and prices down? Here we see another intriguing analogy with Darwinian evolution. Consider once more Charles Darwin's famous Galapagos finches: studies suggest that the finch's evolutionary path takes place conservatively, that is, its underlying body (its "chassis" so to speak) doesn't change that much. Although variations take place throughout the entire bird's body over many generations, there tends to be little selective pressure to change the basics. According to the Galapagos studies, it is the small variations in the beak that appear to be the deciding factor in survivability—especially during period of drought. Putting it another way, the finch's basic "infrastructure" tends to be a reliable component of survival and hence requires little alteration over time. So how does this point relate to the Mustang's development?

Here one might say that Ford had an evolutionary insight. In a critical decision in 1962, Mustang's development team decided to use the relatively reliable chassis and drive train of the earlier Ford model, the Falcon. Evolutionists might therefore call the Falcon a "common ancestor" to the Mustang and to the subsequent Ford models built on the Falcon chassis. The upshot was that the Mustang's base price ($2,368) could be kept relatively low. The car would also earn an enviable reputation for reliability since all the "bugs," common to new models, had already been corrected.

It's intriguing to see how the title of a relatively obscure book, *The Mustangs*, helped one automaker go from a walk to a gallop, eventually making a profitable run across the 1960's economic landscape.

In summary, from bird beaks to body styles, to our own evolutionary journey through time, we live in a wonderful world of creative change, energized by forces of natural and artificial selection contributing to Earth's rainbow of diversity—plants, animals and, (just look around you), a variety of inventions conceived with the miraculous inner workings of the human imagination.

CHAPTER 12

"Then the Sun Came Up"

"The sun is rising. All the green trees are full of birds,
and their song comes up out of the wet bowers of the orchard.
Crows swear pleasantly in the distance,
and in the depths of my soul sits God."
—Thomas Merton

Many readers may recall that popular program on Public Television called "The Power of Myth," featuring a series of interviews by Bill Moyers with the renowned mythologist Joseph Campbell. Among other things we learn the following: although myths may not be factually true or scientifically based, they have nevertheless provided humans with a social infrastructure of meaning necessary for maintaining a cohesive and viable culture over the generations.

Mythological stories, Campbell argued, infused the collective mind with magnified emotional truths as they taught us about such things as the origin of the universe, the origin of humans, the nature of good and evil, and the deep, abiding complexity of the human condition. Campbell's "Power of Myth" has also made it easier for me personally to bridge that canyon of misunderstanding between the evolutionists and creationists. To illustrate, let's take a moment to examine a couple of myths involving a common every day event: the rising of the sun.

Let's begin with one of the Paiute Native American myths entitled "Why the Sun Rises Cautiously," a legend that uses familiar animals and plants to teach young people about socially harmful traits including selfishness, foolishness, and a destructive tendency to solve problems through violence. The main character is an irascible rabbit who desires to get even with the Sun for making his life miserable. You see, poor Cottontail is very upset that he must suffer through the unbearable heat of a Utah summer; attempting to punish the sun (by shooting it with an arrow), Cottontail's plan backfires, creating even more heat than ever and, of course, making everyone more miserable yet. By the time the reader finishes the story, the rabbit has been taught an important lesson while the Sun, now more fearful for its life, he has become much more cautious, more reluctant to rise in the morning:

"He never rises twice in the same place and he always peeks cautiously over the hills before he brings his full body into view. He makes himself so bright, too, that no one could look at him long enough to sight an arrow"[1].

A second illustration, this time from the early Mayan texts again highlights the importance of the rising sun. In this story, we learn about the so called "First People" from the *Popol Vuh*, the sacred text of the Mayan Quiche.

The first Mayans, we learn, were known as "mother-fathers" who lived out their lives in a perpetual dawn, before the advent of days and nights and the predictable movement of the sun across the sky. In a state of constant hunger, the First People lived in what must be described as a nightmare environment, an unnerving twilight zone forcing them to wander aimlessly in semi-darkness with no sense of belonging to a particular place. So what did they do about it?

"In the midst of this suffering, the mother-fathers climbed up a mountain called Place of Advice, and there resolved to turn the mass starvation into an act of penance. Tohil and the other gods were moved at this and responded by ordering Jaguar Quintze and his [Mayan] companions to keep their sacred images safe...And suddenly, the dawn began.

In their happiness Jaguar Quintze and his fellows cried sweetly and burned incense in gratitude. Then the sun itself came up. As it did so, all the birds and animals rose up from the valleys and lowlands and watched the joyous spectacle from the mountain tops. The birds spread their wings to the sun's rays and the first human beings knelt in prayer."[2]

Of course, these two myths—both incorporating the importance of the rising sun—are based on an indisputable fact of nature. After all, the sun does rise, doesn't it? Clearly all one's senses affirm this fact. You can see the sun rise in the east. You can feel it on your skin. Flowers that are warmed by the rising sun release a fragrance; in this sense you can almost smell a rising sun. In addition, birds sense the sun rising in the morning and if you are fortunate enough to enjoy their songs at dawn (as did Thomas Merton, whose quote begins this chapter) you can, as it were, hear the sun coming up. No question: the sun is rising.

The only problem is that the sun is not rising. It's essentially at a standstill in relation to the Earth. The Earth, of course, slowly rotates toward the fixed sun despite the deep sensual, emotional and mythological certainty that the sun is clearly "rising." The scientific explanation, as Galileo unsuccessfully argued to the Catholic Church hierarchy over three hundred and fifty years ago, is an invisible truth lurking in the shadowy world beyond one's senses. Indeed, it is a scientific truth less important on a day-to-day basis than our common perception of witnessing the sun rise each day over and over again.

Still, every once in a while, I try to make an effort to experience the reality of the dawn brightening by envisioning a fixed Sun awaiting this beautiful white and blue sphere as it slowly turns—as our home planet rotates its life-giving atmosphere, plus its mountains, oceans, rivers, cities and all its children along while circling down, down into the light of the sun. It's an interesting sensation, but not the perception that has emotionally energized thousands of years of stories, legends, and time-tested mythologies.

In recognizing the importance of mythological/emotional truths, we can perhaps better understand the creationists' point of view and their passionate argument against evolution. Creationists, I believe, are also immersed in an important and powerful mythological truth: that God literally fashioned the stars, the Earth, and all the animal and plant species pretty much as we see them today. Like the creationists, I too am reluctant to acknowledge that my own ancestry, many many generations ago, descended from a common ancestor of early primates. Indeed, when attending a lecture by a leading creationist, I saw a sign with a simple, but thought-provoking question: "FROM GOO TO YOU??" My ego whispered "no way!" And within that frame of mind, it seemed obvious to me (like the "rising" sun is obvious) that the broad implications of Darwinian evolution were simply too odd, too strange to be true. Indeed, my personal identity and sense of what it means to be human was at stake.

Yet just as I can accept the scientific fact of a moving Earth and a stationary sun, I am convinced that the scientific explanation of evolution— through the exploration and understanding of the fossil record, as well as experiments in genetics and physiology—that biological evolution is the best explanation of how we got here. Thus, I don't "believe" (a religious connotation) in evolution, I accept the scientific explanation as more in line with what likely happened over the past millions of years.

Putting it another way, just like the fixed sun/moving Earth example, we can see human evolution as a kind of invisible truth, a shadowy history painstakingly discovered over a hundred or more years of scientific research. (It's no coincidence that the late Carl Sagan and his wife Ann Druyan titled their book on this subject *Shadows of Forgotten Ancestors: a Search for Who We Are*.)

And yes, every once in a while, I will hold up my hand and think: it is indeed plausible that the curvature of my fingers was, over millions of years, shaped by tree branches, or the arch of my foot was carved upon the African savanna. Years ago, when my appendix was removed, I recall asking the surgeon the purpose of the appendix. It was a "vestigial" organ he said, that was probably important to our purely vegetarian ancestors long ago. (Given the deaths of so many people from ruptured appendices, one would have to wonder why God would consider "designing" humans with such a deadly deficiency.) The surgeon also stressed that I had to take my full dose of antibiotics; if I didn't, I might contribute to the growing problem of antibiotic-resistant strains of bacteria—another illustration of biological change through natural selection.

This conviction was further reinforced when, years ago, my daughter and I were visiting Zion National Park in Utah. While walking down the trail along the Virgin River, we came across an interpretative sign explaining how a local species of snail had changed under the impact of geological forces over millions of years of time. Steering clear of the words "Darwin," "evolution," or "natural selection," the sign simply summed up what science has learned from the fossil record of the snail *Petrophysazionis*:

"Its ancestors probably were pond snails in the old, sluggish Virgin Rivers. Uplift of the land made the river too swift and muddy for their food plants to grow. Food did grow in wet spots on the walls of the deepening canyon. Snails which had happened to have a small shell and larger foot could cling to

the wall better. They survived more often than the others. The environment favored continued reduction in shell and enlargement of foot. Thus the present form is quite different from the ancestral pond snails."

Sounds plausible to me and if there's evolution of snails why not of humans? Indeed, there are times when I'm in a mood, an expansive sensibility as it were, when I feel a deep psychological satisfaction in being part of a long-term evolutionary relationship, a true kinship with all other living things. It's not at all frightening but instead, quite wonderful.

But that's not my day-to-day experience. Just as I go about my mornings enjoying the "fact" of a rising sun, I have no trouble feeling the emotional or mythological truth that Professor Campbell so beautifully outlined years ago. During these moments, I too gravitate toward the power of myth and believe, (with that same comforting conviction as my creationist friends) that "our kind" is essentially unique and my ancestry appears (to me) unrelated to other primates—despite convincing scientific evidence to the contrary.

PART IV:

Values of a Different Order

CHAPTER 13

Looking Deeply

The mountains, I become part of it…
The herbs, the fir tree, I become part of it.
The morning mists, the clouds, the gathering waters,
I become part of it."
—Navajo Chant

In a brief but intriguing essay entitled "Interbeing,"[1] Buddhist teacher and writer Thich Nhat Hanh asks his readers to look deeply at a page of writing and, as an exercise bridging economics and ecology, take a moment now to reflect on what we should be able to "see."

We all know enough economics to be able to see not only the paper and the words, but also there is a publishing company trying to make some revenues and profits. And if there is publishing company, then there would also have to be investors, skilled editors and entrepreneurs just to name a few of the economic contributors. Can you "see" a useful product on the one hand, but also some pollution and deforestation on the other? Undoubtedly, you can "see" a tree as well—perhaps an aspen—because it is often the species used in pulp and paper manufacturing. Nhat Hanh then takes us deeper yet into the page: he asked us to "see" the logger who: "…cut the tree and brought it to the mill…and we see wheat. We know that the logger cannot exist without his daily bread." If we continue to look closely, we should also be able to "see sunshine" and "a cloud":

"Without a cloud, there will be no rain; without rain, the trees cannot grow." Eventually, our journey will take us into an ever-expanding, interconnected universe of widely diverse contributors to the making of the page: "..time, space, the earth, the rain, the minerals in the soil, the sun, the cloud, the river…"

And finally, if we read a page of someone's writing, Nhat Hanh suggests that if we look deeply enough, we can "see" our own perceptions as well: "Your mind is here and mine is also."

CHAPTER 14

Craftsmanship and Salvation

"After a long time, I felt that I had to choose
one way of living or the other...
I took heart again in the old ways
and did what my father had told me to do,
carve [stone] monuments to my people, small monuments.
And then my life changed. A new spirit came back into me
and my life became so great that the sky could not contain it
and the wind and rivers could not move it."
—Gerard Rancourt Tsonakwa

Years ago, I had what one might call a friendly argument with my father. Dad believed that we all move forward by enlarging our individual and collective productivity. He explained that we must grow "two blades of grass where only one grew before." Efficiency and productivity, he said, have not only given us our present standard of living, but will also be the driving force for a better future. What are the tools needed to bring this about? "More investment and improved technology" was his answer.

I have always felt that though his position was generally correct, there was something important missing, but I was never able to put my finger on it. After all, I too value efficiency when I use an automobile to get around. I fly when I need to go long distances. Indeed, what writer would refuse using a computer to speed up their research and become "more and more productive" (as my father would say) in their writing? My misgivings about efficiency and technology always went awry when I objectively observed my own behavior.

But now I believe I know what has been troubling me all those years. It is simply this: modern machinery, technology, and the "cult of efficiency" destroy our age-old psychological need to periodically engage in slow-paced, traditional craftsmanship.

Now when I speak of a lack of craftsmanship, I am not referring to the common complaint today that too many of our products are shoddy and poorly designed, though to some degree this is true. Craftsmanship involves more than that. Craftsmanship implies a particular attitude toward the creative shaping of raw materials. Though outwardly inefficient, inwardly a craftsperson gains a sense of satisfaction, even reverence, for the raw materials and the tools that are skillfully used in the creation of something beautiful, something new.

For writers, the raw material might be simply the richness of words themselves within the vast universe of a particular language. The poet W.H. Auden once wrote that if a person came to him and said, "I have important things to say," he or she would not likely become a poet. But if they said, "I feel like hanging around words, listening to what they say," then Auden felt that this person had a chance to become a writer.

The craft worker in glass savors their glass, stone carvers their stone, quilt makers their fabric, potters their clay, while the furniture craftsman loves his wood and the painter her palate of paint! It's much like a love affair in which the craft person gives birth to some fine art or beautiful artifact. Sometimes the process is sensuous and, at other times, the worker becomes so totally absorbed that the "self" is forgotten—like a child intensively concentrating on play as the hours go by. At other times, it may be more like a form of healing[1]or a spiritual experience.

Indeed, most craftsmen whom I have known feel that there is a "sanctuary" quality to their work. Years ago, Minnesota author Robert Pirsig described so beautifully the experience of simply tuning up a motorcycle: "The first tappet is right on, no adjustment required, so I move on to the next…I always feel like I'm in church when I do this…The gauge is some kind of religious icon and I'm performing a holy rite with it."

Elsewhere in his book, *Zen and the Art of Motorcycle Maintenance*, Pirsig demonstrates that motorcycle maintenance can be an art that leads to an "in-the-present" experience akin to

Zen, where the pain of the past and the anxieties of the future are dissolved as the worker becomes one with his work.

Now consider your friends and relatives: how many true craft workers do you know? Why are there so few? And why hasn't modern technology—especially the widespread use of labor-saving devices—given us that broad margin of leisure time to pursue quality craftwork?

Though I certainly don't know all the reasons, I do know that when we make an obsession out of efficiency and high-speed technologies, we are more likely to diminish our respect for any process that appears to be "inefficient." Furthermore, our high standard of living has given us so many choices that we feel compelled to experience as many possibilities within reach, thus one's "efficient use of time" becomes the order of the day.

And yet, deep down, I suspect that many of us regret the loss of craftsmanship. I feel confident in saying this because I know that most people respond with genuine awe when they see a piece of fine work from the hands of a true craftsperson, such as handmade furniture, blown glass, a beautiful quilt, a painting or a wood-fired handmade clay pot, and yes, even a well-crafted poem. We read, for example, about the craftsmen and women of Appalachia, preservers of blacksmithing, herbal gathering, the craft of stone masonry and the making of handmade musical instruments, just to name a few. We know that somewhere, sometime, we too would like to return to this world of relaxed pace, of deliberateness, and of carefully creating artifacts that reflect what Pirsig called "quality."

Perhaps what we are really seeking is a form of salvation. Some readers may recall that, in the final chapter of his classic, *Walden*, Henry Thoreau suggests that the true craftsman will never die. Our technocrats and ministers of efficiencies would do well to remember Thoreau's account of the Kouroo Artist who strove for perfection in the carving of a walking staff. After many years of working on it—with endless love, patience and complete absorption—he found that his "singleness of purpose and resolution…endowed him…with perennial youth." His friends died, dynasties came and went, and even the polestar in the night sky changed its position! Then at last, when he finally completed his task, the walking-staff,

"...suddenly expanded before the eyes of the astonished artist into the fairest of all creations of Brahma.

He had made a new system in making a staff, a world with full and fair proportions in which, though old cities and dynasties had passed away and fairer and more glorious one had taken their places, the material was pure, and his art was pure. How could the result be other than wonderful?"[2]

CHAPTER 15

Life!

"We belong in this biosphere. We are intimately connected to it.
Our physiology, our psychology.
This planet can actually be a paradise
if we use our intelligence to make it so."
—E.O. Wilson

Not too far from family home in west-central Wisconsin, a small miracle comes our way ever so rarely, rising up and out of a bed of pine needles from our pin-oak and white-pine forest soils. I drop to my knees.

The atmosphere's quiet. The pine-duff layer's soft and moist to the palm of my hand. There in the low morning sun is a fist-sized ring of tiny mushrooms—*Panaeolus foenesecii*—all eleven of them brightened by sunlight beaming through the pine boughs. Each mushroom is vigorous, healthy—full of mirth it seems to me.

Bending down further, I touch one of the mushrooms with my cheek: cool in temperature, rubbery to the skin, it's packed with a new born life force. Closer to the ground now, I'm suddenly aware of strands of spider webs rippling to my right, each fluttering in ruffled waves of rainbow color.

Consider for a moment the favorable confluence of historic and current conditions—biological, geological, meteorological—first to conceive this scene and then to make it into a solid fact: air temperature, night-time humidity, morning sun, perfect pine-duff moisture, plus all the necessary habitat nutrients for mushrooms and spiders. Here was, surrounding me, a delicate combination of chemistry and biology, of DNA imperatives hereby springing up life, now spreading out before me in wind-puffed riffles of color.

Lost in wonder, as if frozen in a dilation of time, I sense old kinships in these familiar forms—an antique creativity summoning up newfound energies. From primordial conditions to such beauty, how, I wonder did the universe do it?

And you and I as well: are we not equal partners of such processes, a species popping up out of rare circumstances, a genuine gift arising from equally improbable events? Are we not, like the mushrooms, exquisite outcomes of evolutionary forces from a truly creative universe cooking up new flavors of recombinant matter, its compounds heated and shaped by a kaleidoscope of chemistries and physical energies over unimaginable quantities of time?

That morning was thus graced by mushrooms and resplendent spider webs fluttering in the wind and a unique Earth-species consciousness invoking feelings of wonder and a sense of planetary preciousness. But there was also a feeling of fear. Indeed who could not also feel a deepening dread that our requisite care toward our home planet has not always been what it should, that Earth has, at times, been so ravaged by human violence, climate destabilization, and ecosystem disfigurement? That our technologies and Earth-consuming appetites have so altered the biosphere that many of those things we hold on to with such affection are now beginning to fade, seep away indeed, slip forever from our fingers.

Consider the planet-wide deforestation and growing number of bleached-out coral reefs. Consider global warming, ozone thinning, and the worldwide shortages of fresh water. Or recall the well-documented amphibian declines and deformities (and the extinction of that beautiful, shimmering Golden Toad of the rainforests of Costa Rica). With any extinction—such as happened with the passenger pigeon, dodo, great auk, heath hen, or dusky seaside sparrow to name a few—one should consider essayist Mark Walter's realization that although death is the end of life, "extinction is the end of birth."[1] Environmental writer Holmes Rolston, arguing along the same lines, writes: "Extinction kills…the soul as well as the body and that to super kill a species is to shut down a story of millennia and leave no future possibilities." [2]

We should also consider the world's bourgeoning population—over seven billion souls with all their basic material needs plus pent-up consumer desires which, if current trends continue, will be a population half again as large within a generation. Consider too the clear-cutting of national forests or Asian mountainsides or the growing severity of worldwide droughts, and elsewhere, torrential rains and tragic mudslides.

Where, one might ask, are our Earth-protecting religions, economics, and politics? Surely many of the earlier spiritual traditions were informed and enriched by a deeper level of ecological consciousness while transmitting to their followers a heightened appreciation not only of the environment, but of a deep, interconnected, harmonic chord of all life. I think, for example, of that great prophetic vision from the Taoist spiritual classic, the *Tao Te Ching*, a vision that beautifully captures all the delicacy, fragility, and indeed the vulnerability of the natural world:

"Those who would take over the earth and shape it to their will, never, I notice, succeed. The earth is like a vessel so sacred that at the mere approach of the profane it is marred and when they reach out their fingers it is gone."[3]

Or consider a passage in the final book of the Bible, a "revelation" startling perhaps to those who may have never considered this book as containing a forceful environmental message: "…that thou should give reward unto thy servants the prophets…and should destroy them which destroy the earth."[4] Or listen to what may be the greatest deep-ecology values proclamation of all time, when the God of Genesis paused to contemplate everything He had created and said that "…it was very good."

Or the Psalmist who cried out so boisterously, (so joyfully!), his praise—not for heaven—but for the natural world:

"O Lord, how manifold are thy works! In wisdom hast thou made them all: The earth is full of thy riches."[5]

Consider too the story of Noah which, according to biologist Calvin DeWitt, is nothing more or less than the world's "first Endangered Species Act." DeWitt reminds his readers that Genesis 6-9 highlights God's command to Noah, a commandment designed to prevent the extinction of all creatures, both economic and uneconomic, no matter what the cost.[6]

And didn't Jesus suggest (as did Henry Thoreau) that we simplify our lives while at the same time, warn us against the "love of money" and the dangers of materialism? The early scriptures of Islam and Hinduism are equally resolute in condemning greed and the worship of material wealth. Buddhists add an additional element of environmental awareness in their view that humans are not separate from the Earth, but intimately part of and interdependent with it. Expanding on the idea of interconnectedness, Zen Buddhist teacher Thich Nhat Hanh asks us to

"Look into the self and discover that it is made only of non-self elements. A human being is made up of only non-human elements. To protect humans, we have to protect the non-human elements—the air, the water, the forest, the river, the mountain, and the animals…Humans can survive only with the survival of other species. This is exactly the teaching of the Buddha, and also the teaching of deep ecology."[7]

Our growing awareness of this Earth/human interdependence may then become a touchstone for our behavior, our lifestyle, and our day-to-day choices. Yet, for some reason, this ancient ecological wisdom has become enfeebled, like a far-off candlelight obscured by great and growing distances—as we race forward embracing the novelty of technology, bottom-line obsessions, and a far-ranging infectious consumerism—making all too many of us unwitting contributors to the slow but steady degradation of our home planet and its countless wonders.

So who is responsible and why? Of course I would like to point my finger outward—toward corrupt governments and greedy transnational corporations—or perhaps blame the advertising and the entertainment industries whose vision of paradise is an ever-expanding consumer culture fueled by increasing profits and exponential growth. Yet, as I must now conclude—I too am co-responsible for some of the environmental destruction, and my finger (if I am honest) more often than not, points right back to me.

CHAPTER 16

Co-Responsibility

"When we try to pick out anything,
we find it hitched to everything else in the universe.
—John Muir

I recall so well that evening when, in the bloom of spring, my wife and I took a leisurely walk down a nearby nature trail. It was all ours—for the seeing, the listening and, here and there, for the sweet smell of the plum blossoms hanging over the path.

On the edge of the trail we found the floral offspring of botanical natives whose ancestors settled here after the last glacier, their living relatives now deeply rooted, as if with a sense of peace and belonging: juneberry, trout lily, and look over there, growing out of the edge of a miniature wetland: fronds of fern unfurling.

Soon we passed a prairie remnant and further on, we discovered marsh marigolds blooming in a sparkling bog. (We have our own flowering golds, like the Sacred Lotus of India, flaring their bright yellows up and out of the mud and into our hearts.) Nearby, skunk-cabbages sprout "elephant ears" for leaves, a yellowthroat scolds us with his "whichity…whichity" while a catbird "meaows" from behind a bush. We pause.

What's that high pitched, haunting trill—as if a thin string of beads had been lofted out of a wet meadow, then transmuted magically into sound? Ah, it's the music of little toads who, like other lovers of this trail, offer their large affections to the efflorescence of the evening, their yearnings to the ripeness of spring.

Turning into a bend along the path we saw something odd, clearly out of place. Somewhere in the many "rooms" of our brain, there's a recognition center alerting us to oddness or novelty which, like an unexpected Special News Bulletin interrupting soothing music, immediately arouses our curiosity. The strange object was white, a little less than a foot in length, and surprisingly straight and as we got closer, curiosity modulated into confoundedness. Nothing in nature that I could recall is so smooth, so precisely linear.

The mystery object was, of course, a plastic straw that had been thoughtlessly tossed into a wetland. My wife fished it out. It was mostly white, but upon closer inspection, it also had a thin red stripe down one side and a yellow one down the other. Some of the plastic had been chewed off and discarded. "Not for me" some critter must have thought to himself. Nor for us either—this artifact from the world of fast food, this offspring of chemical engineers, oil wells, tankers, pipelines, machine extrusion processes and robotic packing machines.

Oh, the delicacy of the day, its hushed, prayer-like moment—now so rudely interrupted! Instantly, from eye to brain, feeling of disgust entered the judgmental part of my mind and soon rippled down into the body, briefly diminishing the color, the music, the wonder and sparkle of the moment.

Days later, I would reflect on that evening. I would wonder why I usually accept, with little thought or feeling, much greater disfigurement of the natural world as I drive through our cities and suburbs. Or, for example, when I do not let it bother me very much when we dispose of our trash, week by week, each plastic bag destined for some invisible landfill.

I confess to living day to day mentally predisposed to destructive states of denial, and also to a gross numbing of my ecological and aesthetic sensibilities, of accepting wide-ranging forms of social and environmental blight as normal: light pollution, exhaust pollution, subtle chemical pollution, endless sprawl—and also doing very little to prevent the cancers, the children's asthma, or the mercury in fish, to name just a few transgressions of my deeply held values.

If I could only be more aware of my actions and what I am consuming, I would understand that I too am co-responsible for the poisons, for the animal and plant extinctions, for global deforestation and the planet's slow but inexorable climate change. As Buddhist writer Thich Nhat Hanh put it:

"...the most important precept of all is to live in awareness, to know what is going on, not only here, but there. For instance, when you eat a piece of bread, you may choose to be aware that our famers, in growing the wheat, use chemical poisons a little too much. Eating the bread, we are somehow co-responsible for the destruction of our ecology."[1]

Lately I have also been thinking about my driving habits. Consider the fact that my wife and I drove to the nature trail. Each gallon of gas, when combined with atmospheric oxygen, adds nearly twenty pounds of carbon dioxide into the air. Thus on a recent fill-up, I used some 10 gallons for some 320 miles which would translate into approximately 200 pounds of carbon dioxide added to the atmosphere. My yearly automobile CO_2 "footprint" is around 3 tons (10,000 miles @ 32 miles per gallon). Other pollutants from driving our cars may affect forests thousands of miles away or more locally in the form of urban ozone affecting adult and childhood asthma. Oil spills from pipelines, ships, and deep water oil rigs (such as the tragic BP oil leak into the Gulf of Mexico) are also part of a vast array of related collateral damage related to our excessive consumption of oil.

Sometimes when I complete a litany of social and environmental damage of driving, a student will ask if I don't "feel guilty." I try not to because guilt often dissipates over time and is eventually replaced by a comfortable state of moral amnesia. Instead, I believe that the principle of co-responsibility should become a tool for understanding, a kind of force-field for truth, in the same spirit perhaps as the great religious insights. As poet Matthew Arnold once wrote commenting on the "Sermon on the Mount" in the New Testament:

"Jesus," he said, was not engaging in "stiff and stark external commands," but in lessons that "have the most soul in them; because these can best sink down into our soul, work there, set up an influence, and form habits of conduct."[2]

Likewise, the principle of co-responsibility can also assist us in gaining insight and understanding as we search for environmentally sound decisions and ecologically healthy lifestyles.

Another example comes from my own home economy involving a remodeling decision we made a number of years ago. In the summer of 1991 my wife and I put down new kitchen flooring, and on the advice of our local building materials supplier, we dutifully purchased (without checking for certification of sustainable forestry practices) the recommended underlayment: thin, smooth sheets of plywood called lauan. Lauan is one of the varieties of Philippine mahogany of genus *Shorea*. These four-by-eight foot panels originated from trees that can reach a height of one hundred and fifty feet with a circumference of eighty-five feet or more.

I can easily visualize these ancient forests—from their underground roots to their overarching canopies—forests replete with unique, diverse, and fully functioning ecosystems including, of course, wonderful groves of these silent mahogany behemoths, trees larger in circumference than even the great redwoods of California. (It would, for example, take some twenty children to put their collective arms around a single trunk of the largest of these giants.) Such an image by itself should have given us pause in purchasing lauan mahogany for our subflooring.

Imagine our shock and dismay when, a few months after the floor was completed, we discovered that the Philippine island of Leyte, a major source of lauan, had suffered massive flooding, death, and destruction traced to large-scale clear-cutting of mahogany trees from the island's mountainous slopes. With little foliage to break the energy of some six inches of rain from tropical hurricane Thelma, plus the absence of dense root systems that would normally anchor the topsoil, an estimated twenty-one million cubic yards of earth washed down the mountainsides on the fifth of November, 1991, creating a ten foot high wall of water, mud, and debris—all cascading into Leyte's Anilao River valley—and then continued to rage through and scour the heart of the island's largest city, Ormoc.

By the end of the week, some six thousand residents had died, tens of thousands were homeless, and millions of dollars worth of crops had been ruined. Two days after the flood, New York Times reporter Seth Mydans pieced together various on-the-site observations and commented: "residents of Ormoc said the floodwaters, preceded by a great roar, uprooted trees, flushed cars down the streets and ripped wooden houses from their foundations."

But why did this happen? When Lito Osmena, governor of the nearby island of Cebu, presented his explanation, I wondered if our family too didn't play some small role in this tragedy:

"...The forests are gone and I guess over-logging is one of the major causes... That area gets several typhoons a year but they never resulted in something like this, and I think it is because the forests are gone. Illegal logging, with the complicity of local politicians and military officers, has recently become recognized as a major environmental problem in the Philippines. Forest cover is being stripped from the hillsides and erosion is degrading the land."[3]

After the flood and mudslides, other eye-witnesses reported the following:

"The captain of an inter-island vessel, Porfirio Labugnay, interviewed in Cebu, said: 'I saw bodies and animals, cows, pigs, and household appliances floating in the sea off Ormoc city.'

'People were in a panic,' said Demetria Go, a 48 year-old resident. 'They were scampering into the streets. Some children climbed up trees yelling for help. People were screaming as they ran from their houses." Like individual drops of rain—dollar by dollar by dollar—these monetary pulses when added up, swell into a powerful river—a great global force that's beyond any individual's or single group's control. Add in greed, poverty, political corruption. Add in clear-cutting shrouded from view and muffled by distance, and you now have a confluence of events ripe for human and biological tragedy on a massive scale.

Leyte's flood was not an "act of God," but truly an act of humans—consumers, loggers, politicians, and all the persuasive advocates for unregulated free trade. Indeed, after the tragedy of Leyte, I understood for the first time what author Helena Norberg-Hodge meant when she wrote:

"The ever-expanding scope and scale of the global economy obscures the consequences of our actions: In effect, our arms have been so lengthened that we no longer see what our hands are doing. Our situation exacerbates and furthers our ignorance, preventing us from acting out of compassion and wisdom."[4]

After the Leyte disaster, I am also able to better understand what environments call an ecological footprint, a concept, like co-responsibility, that forces us to recognize our own social and environmental responsibilities beyond one's immediate visual space. Your ecological footprint, for example, is defined as the amount of land you require for your individual housing, transportation, waste disposal, food production and distribution, the manufacture of your consumer products, and so forth. Rough calculations indicate that each North American, on average, uses between eleven and thirteen acres of productive land to meet their material requirements.[5] (Comparatively, an average person in India uses only one acre.) After Leyte, the environmentalist's observation, "if everyone on Earth had the same level of consumption as North Americans, we would need three planet Earths to satisfy our demand" seems not only plausible, but might well be a reminder in which we can, as Matthew Arnold wrote, "…sink down into our soul, work there, set up an influence and form habits of conduct."

In thinking about these issues, I sometimes feel overwhelmed—as if we were all submerged in an ocean of commercialism, drowning in a for-profit culture. It's everywhere! The bottom line is… well, "The Bottom Line." It's in our language, it's in our schooling philosophy ("go to school to get a good job"), and it's in nearly every media niche saturated with commercialized entertainments along their daytime and nighttime flood-tide of marketing messages.

It's in the hourly report: "The Dow Jones Averages are up" (or down). It's in politics bought and sold, it's in retail stores that never close, it's in electronic televangelists promoting above all, material prosperity. Indeed, excessive materialism seems to be deeply embedded in many of our work and family issues: stress, debt, overwork, road rage, loss of free time, the deterioration of community, teenage self-image issues, eating disorders, and of course, environmental alienation.

In conclusion, it's likely that we all, in one way or another, contribute to this pervasive materialist culture and are thus co-responsible for many of the often invisible "externalities" which, when revealed, sadden the heart and wound the soul; forces, like the great flood of Leyte, that diminish creation and irreversibly damage the beauty and diversity of our fragile planet.

CHAPTER 17

The Coming Repair Age

"Great trouble comes
From not knowing what is enough
Great conflict arises from wanting too much."
—Lao Tzu

Have you ever broken your glasses? No, not the lens, but the thin plastic section in the middle of the frame? Surely it happens to people now and then, for it has recently happened to me. If your frames did break, did you try to repair them? Were you successful?

My broken glasses got me thinking about the importance of mending skills, particularly in relation to our current and future economic situation. I came to the conclusion that one element of environmental stewardship would involve putting some of our energies into the art of repair and maintenance.

It's no secret that, sooner or later, the world's energy supplies will dwindle and that Earth's once large supply of raw materials will become increasingly scarce. Common sense tells us that there simply must be an end to our wastefulness and that we cannot continue our gross consuming habits for the long run. Thus there seems to be but two fundamental choices: the first is simply "more of the same," that is unsustainable economic growth and eventual economic collapse.

The second choice is to move toward an ecological consciousness that includes an ethic of repair and maintenance. It would consist of an economy which sustains itself on what we have today, with opportunities for new and durable inventions from time to time.

I hope we select the second alternative—to consciously choose to save those things that are most useful and then keep them in sound working condition for ourselves and for posterity. This environmental consciousness begins with an appreciation for the elegance of repair and the ritual of maintenance.

I began to understand this point more clearly while reading an intriguing book entitled *Craftsmen of Necessity*, by Christopher Williams. Consider the following quote:

"The indigenous societies of the world gear their lives to a small assortment of deeply loved goods, gently made, carefully used and lovingly repaired."[1]

When I first read this passage, I was reminded of a small stool I came across in Africa, one that had been carefully crafted by a traditional Kikuyu artisan of Kenya. No doubt that this lovely artifact—with its circular, concave seat and gay, though somewhat distorted faces on each of its three legs—was the work of a true artist. But what I also admired was its exquisite repair work: small pieces of broken wood carefully sewn together with thin copper wire, the ends of which were artfully coiled in patterns of concentric circles contrasting wonderfully with the dark stain of the smooth wood. Where breaks had to be bridged, there were short, flat lengths of scrap copper tightly binding the broken pieces. Magnificent!

Imagine somebody taking an interest in preserving this artifact over the years. These handsome repairs may even have been made over a hundred years or more. I don't know.

I do know that the Gurungs (a traditional tribal community of central Nepal), have also shown equal ingenuity. Indeed, a Gurung repairer's reputation may well span generations:

"The Gurung's compulsive resourcefulness is almost an embarrassment to the casual observer. Axes, ploughs and digging tools are used until they are worn beyond recognition. The village blacksmiths then reincarnate the stubs into another generation of tools and utensils; Aama can recall the lineage of successive incarnation of each of her pots, ladles and hoes..."[2]

Do the above descriptions of ingenious improvisations, artful repair, and meticulous maintenance describe our future? I believe so, though surely we have a ways to go to match the Kikuyu or Gurung's art and skill of mending and maintenance. Yet, putting artfulness aside, some of us have made impressive progress when it comes to quality maintenance and longevity of our possessions.

I think, for example of Irv Gordon of East Patchogue New York who has meticulously maintained his Volvo purchased new in 1966. Though one might question his car's contribution to atmospheric CO_2, most people would be impressed with the total mileage Erv has been able to squeeze out of one meticulously maintained vehicle. As of this writing, Gordon's little red Volvo has travelled over two million eight hundred thousand miles. No doubt Erv Gordon will someday be able to pass his car onto another generation—a Gurung at Heart!

In another example, I know someone who "repairs" and maintains prairie remnants, defining his work in terms of restoration, and the "healing" of native natural areas. He too loves the rituals of maintenance, including his setting off prairie fires in the spring.

These are just a couple examples of the harbingers of a new maintenance ethic, prophets of the coming repair age. Incidentally, I did surprise myself when I temporarily fixed my broken frame. Super glue works pretty well as does my new favorite—5-minute epoxy. But my repair wasn't particularly elegant, nothing like the mending of the stool or as beautiful as a restored prairie.

No, most of us need to learn and practice the skills of repair and maintenance—a seemingly lost art in our fast-paced, consumer driven society. It will surely be something new for many of us, we who are so accustomed to our wasteful ways. Or, we might view the coming repair age as simply returning home—safely—after the big party.

CHAPTER 18

Quartet

"We are like a musician who faintly hears a melody
deep within the mind,
but not clearly enough to play it through."
—Thomas Berry

Like the meadowlark's "role" in the natural scheme of things, or the mushrooms, or the web-weaving spiders, have you ever wondered: what is our part in the "music" of the cosmos, what is our role in the harmony of nature's variations on a theme? Indeed, how might we describe our special part in the ensemble of life on Earth?

If you allow me to indulge in one final metaphor, I suggest that our species' format might be likened to a quartet involving four equal interlacing voices representing our past, present, and future possibilities.

For inspiration, I pull out some of my favorite recordings: the string quartets by Beethoven. How amazing these works are, how entrancing! Four players, four instruments, four tonal lines weaving in and out, intertwining harmonies, disharmonies, now floating heavenward, now earthward and back again. Eventually the musical moment deepens until, after a variegated journey though time and space, the voices settle into a peaceful resolution.

In his fifteenth quartet the listener can enjoy a "Song of Thanksgiving," a musical psalm as it were, composed in 1825 to celebrate the composer's recovery from a long and debilitating illness. In this movement, Beethoven walks the listener through a variety of tonalities; his mood is joyous, awake and, above all, supremely grateful for the forces that gave him a sense of life, health, and revitalization of his creative powers. "With a sense of renewed strength," he wrote on the original manuscript, and later near the end he writes: "…with the most intimate feeling."

So if our species' metaphor is a quartet, what do the four voices represent?

Perhaps one of the melodic parts might represent that dimension of our species' cosmological and biological past. Indeed, each of us contains atomic structures formed in the life-and-death rhythm of countless stars. In addition, each of our cells' DNA is packed with deep-time animal histories—from Cambrian chordates, to amphibians, from reptiles to fist-sized mammals, from arboreal apes to savanna-dwelling *Homo erectus*. Evidence of our common past in contained in our shape, our organs, our limbs, our "animal" senses—indeed, in the very structure of our brains. Surely this part of our "music" is still with us and even today plays an important role in our psychological and physical well-being. Those people, who live in bubbles of man-made technologies, may find it difficult to reconnect to this part of themselves and experience what biologist E.O. Wilson calls "biophilia"—defined as an innate attraction to and psychological need for bonding with nature, its landscapes, ecosystems, and its communities of plants and animals.

Cocooned in our cars or cooped up in our classrooms or office cubicles, or simply consuming hours of our waking day wandering through an unnatural wasteland of prepackaged electronic entertainments, we may be allowing our vital connection to nature to atrophy, and thereby suffer from a peculiar loneliness, a vague unsettling or alienation, or even a form of depression.

Children, especially, need large chunks of un-programmed, spontaneous time in nature to discover landscape niches, to "practice the wild," as poet Gary Snyder once called it. Author David Abram expresses so well the depths and delights of this neglected component of fully utilizing our fine-tuned sensory system in his book *Becoming Animal*,[1] while essayist Dian Ackerman highlights the healing aspects of immersing ourselves in the natural world:

"We need a lively, bustling natural world so we can stay healthy…We need it to feel whole. We evolved as creatures

knitted into the fabric of nature, and without its intimate truths, we can find ourselves unraveling."[2]

Biophilia is a new term paralleling older themes in writings that go as far back as second-century naturalist Pliny the Elder (who, for example, believed that the only virtuous life as one lived in balance—ratio—with nature), the Bible, as well as writers such as William Wordsworth, John Muir, Aldo Leopold and, as we noted earlier, Henry David Thoreau. Recall, for instance, Thoreau's comment that "there could be no black melancholy to him who lives in the midst of nature and has his senses still."[3] And what better definition of Wilson's biophilia than Thoreau's description of an inner musical counterpoint between himself and his feathery neighbors in the "Sounds" chapter of Walden:

"Instead of singing like the birds, I silently smiled at my incessant good fortune. As the sparrow had its trill, sitting on the hickory before my door, so had I my chuckle or suppressed warble which he might hear out of my nest...I am no more lonely than a single mullein or dandelion in a pasture, or a bean leaf, or sorrel, or a horse-fly, or a humblebee."[4]

Consider too Wisconsin teacher and naturalist Aldo Leopold. Despite Leopold's training as a "bottom-line" forester, his understanding and appreciation of the natural world would eventually evolve toward values beyond economic utility, even beyond the aesthetic dimension: "Our ability to perceive quality in nature" he wrote, "begins, as in art, with the pretty. It expands through successive stages of the beautiful to values as yet uncaptured by language."[5] Like Thoreau, Leopold would become more and more critical of an economic system geared to short-term gain only while tragically out of balance with ecological values.

As a writer and conservationist, John Muir also dedicated his energies to "do something for nature and make the mountains glad," and like Thoreau, Muir could dissipate despondence and depression by taking periodic pilgrimages into the wild. My own favorite quote however is not from Muir's legendary mountain or glacial hikes, but from a moment of relaxed repose while sitting between two rivers and flowering grassland:

"*Here is a calm so deep, grasses cease waving...wonderful how completely everything in wild nature fits into us, as if truly part and parent of us. The sun shines not on us, but in us. The rivers flow not past, but through us, thrilling, tingling, vibrating every fiber and cell of the substance of our bodies, making them glide and sing."*[6]

In the same spirit as these American naturalists, major Judeo-Christian figures—Moses, John the Baptist, Jesus—apparently felt that same urge to seek spiritual nourishment in wilderness settings including pilgrimages to sites connected to rivers, lakes, mountains, and deserts.

For the Ecumenical Patriarch of the Eastern Orthodox Church, Bartholomew I, any destruction of the natural world should be considered a sin. Bartholomew, in the spirit of the poet-naturalists, says that "human beings and environment form a seamless garment of existence, a complex fabric that we believe is fashioned by God."[7]

This brings us to the second musical line in our quartet: our capacity to realize a spiritual potential, that is to experience, as Christians might define it, the "energy of the Holy Spirit," or, as Martin Luther King Jr. reminded his followers: the practice of offering unconditional love—even to your "enemies" —no matter what the consequence to yourself.[8] Or the Taoist's concept of experiencing the supreme Tao: "Wonderful, perfect…All life comes from it. It wraps everything with its love as in a garment…I do not know its name."[9]

In Buddhism, it might be described as "Great Love and Compassion" (*mahakaruna*), while in Islam, "the infinite mercy of Allah." Related to this is Islam's Golden Rule, ("No one of you is a believer until he desires for his brother that which he desires for himself"[10]) a variation on a familiar theme that can be found in Christianity and Judaism as well as in the writings of Confucius.

"While we know not definitely what the ultimate purport of life is," wrote the Zen Buddhist, D.T. Suzuki, "there is something in it that makes us feel infinitely blessed in the living of it and remain quite contented with it in all its evolution."[11] The spiritual component is also the mystical awareness ballooning up and around American poet Walt Whitman described in his poem, "Song of Myself":

"Swiftly arose and spread around me the peace and knowledge that pass all argument of the earth…And I know the spirit of God is the brother of my own."[12]

Next, consider another quality of our species: the role of traditional culture, the third musical line of our quartet. Our cultural heritage is the learned social sphere that surrounds us from birth, influencing us day to day, year by year, while informing each of us not only how to survive, but how to enjoy a richer existence. Assuming that much (but not all) of the culture's influence is positive, it can also assist us in diminishing our ego while making it possible to grow through family and friendship intimacies as well as through wider circles of social belonging.

Traditional cultural practices are often finely tuned to local landscapes. Similar to the time-tested ecological fit of native species in their particular habitats, traditional cultures also fit into their specific landscapes and, over time, evolve sustainable economic practices. For thousands of years, horticultural and hunter/gatherer cultures integrated ecological ethics through ceremony, cosmologies, mythologies, taboos, stories, songs, dances, food sharing and other customs. Thus we discover unique and sustainable culturescapes in all their variation and richness.

Consider, for example, the traditional horticulturists and herders of Ladakh, a district in northern India, beautifully described in Helena Norbert-Hodge's study, *Ancient Futures*. In reading her book, the reader discovers about a way of life that has maintained an exquisite balance between a particular people and its available local resources, a balance that has been aided and informed by Buddhist practices including the principles of interdependence, co-responsibility, and a reverence for life.

As a professional economist, I was impressed learning about Ladakh's age-old adaptability over the many generations, and its success in solving fundamental economic survival problems. The example of Ladakh has thus become for me a useful, indeed, an inspiring touchstone to compare and contrast with my own consumer driven, free-market economy. For Ladakh is not a growth economy, but a stable economy, successfully fitting into the natural limits of its boundaries without radically altering the land or destroying its resource base. Ladakhians live in an environment that provides not only basic economic sustenance, but a landscape where one can find plant and animal "teachers" as well as time-honored sacred sites—storied places of love and belonging.

In contrast, global capitalism tends to reshape the land, without a sense of the sacred and without the love and belonging. Not fitting into a local landscape, large-scale industries, (often with the assistance of large-scale governments) may reconfigure landscapes based on the dictates of unlimited growth and profit—giving rise to industrial farmers, strip miners, stream straighteners, road wideners, wetland drainers, and forestry clear-cutters, to name a few.

Within the modern urban sectors of Ladakh, the author of *Ancient Futures* describes some of the tragic environmental and psychological consequences of the impact of Western globalization, education, and even tourism. In the span of only a couple of decades, she witnessed a perplexing increase in relative poverty, social isolation, greater levels of air and water pollution, disempowerment of women, and an increase in ethnic tensions between Buddhists and Muslims, especially in the Ladakh's capital city of Leh.

As once traditional cultures are undermined by the seduction of modernization that's beamed out by the ubiquitous global media—billboards, movies, radio, TV—young people feel that irresistible tug toward Western consumptive lifestyles. Shunning traditional ways, this generation is, unfortunately, not well adapted to the modern economy either as they lack the income to keep pace with Western material desires. These drifters are floating, like "Hungry Ghosts," (as they are called in some countries) in a kind of no-man's land. They tend to be, in a phrase, unsuccessful "two-worlders," stuck somewhere between traditionalism and Western "middleclassism." Without roots in either world and without a reliable religious/cultural infrastructure of meaning and belonging (yet eager for the fruits of consumerism), many become resentful and not surprisingly, may fall prey to scapegoating and militant propaganda.

After reading Norberg-Hodge's account of Ladakh's recent stresses and struggles, I felt that we too, while seemingly integrated into a modern consumer economy, may also suffer from some of the same social and psychological symptoms of being uprooted from land and culture and therefore may experience similar symptoms of alienation:

"And so we have before us the spectacle of unprecedented prosperity," poet Wendell Berry once wrote, "…but in a land of degraded farms, forests, ecosystems, and water-sheds, polluted air, failing families, and diminishing communities."[13]

In fact, any society that trades in a balanced ecological and spiritual ethic for one fueled by economic discontent will find itself severed from its roots, and can easily lose that vital "sense of place." Perhaps it is not too late to begin to rediscover one's own cultural and ecological rootedness, to become intimate with our landscapes and watersheds; to learn, if we can, the land's histories, its stories, and songs and to be acquainted with its geology, its plants and animals. And revive, if possible, the local crafts and folklore, the rituals to help us become "native to our place," to feel nourished, like the traditional people of Ladakh, by the land while enjoying that comforting sense of love and belonging.

In his book *Miracle Under the Oaks*, author William Stevens describes some of the accomplishments, disappointments, and joys of a Chicago-based prairie restoration group. In reading about their experiences, I can make out the beginnings of a true local culture, informed by common purpose and group solidarity, united by rituals (for example, the burning of the prairie in the springtime), and guided by "elders" (those who've mastered the art and science of ecological restoration). In a revealing comment, one member of this group said:

"What's happening here is that Europeans are finally becoming Americans. We are developing an intimate relationship with this continent, and the landscapes of the continent, and we're doing it using the science of ecology, a product of our own culture."[14]

There is no reason why one cannot strive to become what might be called a successful two-worlder, by not only becoming rooted in one's locality, but also by embracing the fruits of past and present human accomplishments: the sciences, literature, music, arts, languages, medicine, etc. The fourth element in this chapter's musical quartet theme will thus be called the *liberal learning dimension.*

This "modernity" theme would also include the following: a tolerance of differentness, the spirit of free inquiry, plus an appreciation of democracy as well as the selected use of technologies which have proven to be democratic, humane, ethical, and sustainable. These contributions—comprising of the fruits of past and present civilizations—are thus our species' relatively new source of kinship and belonging, shining brightly, as it were, through both time and space. Despite human greed and destructiveness, despite unpardonable violence, the great achievements of humankind make me glad to be a member of that quirky tribe, *Homo sapiens*.

The recording of the quartet is, for now, over. It's time for bed. For a few minutes, I linger about—feeling strangely happy—happy for this music and also happy to have heard the song of a Meadowlark earlier in the day or for the Bluebird who dived into the grass outside my window; happy for the lowly mushrooms and the towering pines, for the sound of raindrops or, in the early dawn, for the virtuosity of sunbeams.

Happy too for my own consciousness and now, stepping outside into the cool, fresh, night air—happy to see a half-moon beaming softly to the night from behind a distant pine.

May I too learn to sing and to listen well, to treasure our music's intertwining and be thankful for each of its variegated voices? May I also enjoy a deeper connectedness to this existence, its pulse and mystery and to its everlasting ensemble—to keep humming along, mindful of the music—indeed, a "Song of Thanksgiving."

Surely Beethoven must have sensed this. Even the Old Testament psalmist made it clear: "That I may publish with the voice of thanksgiving and tell of all thy wondrous works"[15] and the Zen master who wrote so simply, so powerfully:

"When my life opens up very clearly, I can't help from the depths of my heart, wanting to bow."[16]

Coda

DEDUCTING THOREAU'S SHOES

"This curious world which we inhabit is more wonderful than it is convenient; more beautiful than it is useful; it is more to be admired and enjoyed than used." –Henry Thoreau

Recently while taking my morning walk, I caught a glimpse of a man who was (and here I'm afraid many of you will not believe me), none other than the great naturalist writer (and economic prophet) Henry David Thoreau.

Though he passed by me quickly, I noticed that his head was down, looking, in fact, somewhat depressed as he strode by in his heavy shoes and long, black overcoat. Where was that cheerful, inquisitive naturalist, poking into this, listening to that, letting nothing get by his legendary powers of observation? Something, I believe was bothering the man.

I felt duty-bound to catch up and ask: "Is it really you, the Henry David Thoreau, pencil-maker, surveyor, poet, essayist, and natural historian who retreated to Walden Pond over a hundred and fifty years ago?"

"Yes, yes," he said, while giving me a strange look, as if she were perturbed about something.

"Anything wrong?" I inquired.

"Since you asked, I'll tell you. To begin with, the other day I stepped into one of your Main Street taverns. The owner invited me in to check out her new high definition plasma television. 'At 60 inches, it's the biggest television in town,' she said.

'The customers say it's awesome.'"

"I then sat down to watch what she called her favorite 'soap opera' and what seemed to be a loud and I might add, annoying quiz show. 'Terrible! Terrible!' I then told her, 'I'm sorry if I sound critical Miss, but these programs confirm, for me at least, that the mass of men lead lives of quiet desperation.'"

"Henry, you've really got to be careful what you say to people," I said.

"Well, that wasn't all. That evening I returned to the same establishment and asked if anyone would like to go for a walk to listen to the spring peepers and watch the rising of the full moon. But no one seemed interested. In fact, one young gentleman glared at me and said, "Get real dude. Like, can't you see there's a game on?"

"I felt sorry for him," Thoreau continued. "It seems to me that a stereotyped but unconscious despair is concealed even under what are so-called games and amusements of mankind. Your cars, your television programs and movies, and what you call 'computers' make things worse! Are they not all merely pretty toys which distract our attention from more serious things?"

"Most people," I said, "might argue that they are the most important advances since you wrote *Walden* in 1854. Come on Henry, weren't you awed by that high-definition TV?"

"Technically, my friend, it was impressive. But if all you watch are those puerile programs, then it would seem to me that your plasma tele-machines are nothing more than an improved means to an unimproved end. As for your automobiles, see how they've disfigured, even destroyed what was once a lovely landscape! Everywhere you look—cars, roads, parking lots! I ask you, who is in control, you or your cars?"

Continuing his train of thought, Thoreau added: "If I had the opportunity to revise *Walden*, I would pay more attention to how the commercial interests, especially in their advertising, have conspired to keep people—what should I say?—'stunted,' where they remain stuck in their juvenile larval state. The commercial interests clearly do not want people to grow up. One does not have to look far to see men and women wasting their lives with such toys and childish amusements."

"Perhaps you're right," I said, "but most people here say that at least we have an excellent school system, and when the kids graduate they can work at the local Walmart or the Mega-Mall in Minneapolis."

However as I spoke, my friend was wistfully looking off into a distant woods. He then gestured toward the trees and quietly said, "Sir, what is important is a constant intercourse with nature and the contemplation of natural phenomena. The discipline of schools or businesses can never impart such serenity of mind."

Turning to me again, he asked sharply: "Why do you need megamalls, or Walmarts?"

"Americans love to shop, I mean ... er, we purchase products that make our lives more interesting, more comfortable."

"I'm not so sure," he countered. "Many of the so-called comforts of life are not only dispensable, but positive hindrances to the elevation of mankind. Believe me sir, you don't need shopping malls."

Changing the subject, I asked if he had seen any meadowlarks about, as they seemed to be losing ground. Bullfrogs as well, even our fireflies and leopard frogs were diminishing in numbers, I told him.

"No, I haven't. Indeed I am very sad to hear about such things. As for me, I am still searching for a hound, a bay horse, and a turtledove. Any chance you might have seen one of these?"

Actually, that morning I had seen a pair of mourning doves on a telephone wire, but I don't think that's what he meant. Besides, I didn't want to bring up the subject of long-distance communication, recalling what he said in *Walden* about the magnetic telegraph that would connect Maine to Texas. "Maine and Texas, it may be, have nothing important to communicate," he wrote. Likewise, I didn't want to bring up cell phones or the topic of social networking, so popular among youth and adults too. I have a feeling I know what he would say.

Then Thoreau asked me what I did for a living. "I'm an economist," I said. "I teach a little, write a little, sort of like what you did years ago."

"You're an economist? Perhaps you are responsible for the

federal income tax which appears to be something new since I wrote *Walden*.

"Well, yes, I suppose economists had something to do it, along with the politicians."

With that, my friend began to explain what had been on his mind, a worry that had distracted him to the degree that he wasn't able to write or even enjoy his walks anymore.

The government is after me," he confessed. "They said that I would have to pay back-taxes on the income that I have earned over these many years—from the sales of *Walden*, as well as from my poetry and essays."

"Tough problem," I said, "But I've got an idea that might work. Next time you see the tax man, explain to him that you're planning to take a "Poet's Deduction" the amount of which would be equal to what you have spent over the years."

"Wait a moment. You're going much too fast for me. What's a Poet's Deduction? I confess though, I do like the sound of it."

"Okay. Take your shoes, Henry—"

"What do my shoes have to do with my taxes?" he interrupted.

"Don't you see? The cost of your shoes is a legitimate business deduction, like the cost of say, a farmer's tractor or barn. Do you remember when you wrote: 'How many a poor immortal soul have I met well-nigh crushed and smothered under its load, creeping down the road of life, pushing before it a barn seventy-five by forty, its Augean stables never cleansed?'"

"Yes, first chapter of *Walden*, I believe."

"What you didn't realize is that those uncleaned Augean stables are not completely bad: a farmer is allowed a deduction for all his business expenses, his barn included."

"Hmmm … I think I'm beginning to understand."

"You might argue that anything a poet, a philosopher, indeed anything a writer like yourself purchases is part of what one might say: 'operating their business.' There is no separation between a poet's lifestyle in general and his or her writing in particular—those things from which they earn their income. Therefore all your expenditures can be deducted from your writing income. Yes, Henry David Thoreau, you can deduct your shoes—and everything else, too."

With that my friend began to brighten up.

"Extraordinary idea, sir. I'll pursue your Poet's Deduction next time I see the taxman. But now I must take my leave. I see it is the waking-day's crepuscular hour, my favorite time of day. Thank you and good-bye."

He sauntered off. (Did I detect a smile on his face?) I saw him go down the road a ways, then head off into a nearby meadow, engrossed with something, he stopped, took out his journal and, I'm pleased to report, began writing again.

Notes

Chapter 1

1. E.F. Schumacher, *Small Is Beautiful* (New York: Perennial Library, 1973), 54-55.
2. Karl Taro Greenfield, "The Battle Hymn of Bill McKibben," *Bloomberg Businessweek*, Feb. 2013, 54-59.

Chapter 4

1. Henry David Thoreau, *Walden* (New York: Bramall House, 1951), 19.
2. Ibid.
3. Henry David Thoreau, *The Journal of Henry David Thoreau*,(New York: Dover, 1962), 446-447.
4. Henry David Thoreau, *Walden* (New York: Bramall House, 1951), 67.
5. Ibid., 67.
6. Ibid., 66.
7. Ibid., 51.
8. Ibid., 148.
9. Ibid., 337.
10. Walter Harding, *The Days of Henry David Thoreau* (New York: Dover, 1982), 286.
11. Henry David Thoreau, *Walden* (New York: Bramall House, 1951), 106.
12. Henry David Thoreau, *The Journal of Henry David Thoreau*, (New York: Dover, 1962), 224.
13. Henry David Thoreau, *The Natural History Essays* (Salt Lake City: Peregrine Smith, Inc, 1980), 135.
14. Henry David Thoreau, *Walden* (New York: Bramall House, 1951), 86.
15. Ibid., 45.

Chapter 6

1. Norman Ware, *The Industrial Worker 1840-1860* (Gloucester, MA: Peter Smith, 1959), viii.
2. Ibid., 45.
3. Duncan T. Moore, "No Rust in Rochester," *New York Times*, Feb. 2, 2012.

Chapter 9

1. George A. Sheehan, *Dr. Sheehan on Running* (Mountain View, CA: World Publishers, 1975), 190.
2. Eugen Herrigel, *Zen in the Art of Archery* (New York: Vintage, 1971), 41.

Chapter 10

1. C.S. Lewis, *The Four Loves* (New York: Harcourt Brace Jovanovich, 1960), 56-57.
2. Lao Tzu, *The Way of Life*, trans. by R.B. Blakney (New York: American Library, 1955), 56.
3. K.L. Reichelt, *Meditation and Piety in the Far East* (New York: Harper & Bros., 1954), 56.
4. Tsonakwa and Yolaikia, *Legends in Stone, Bone, and Wood* (Minneapolis: Arts and Learning Services Foundation, 1986), 14.
5. Ibid., 14.
6. Ibid., 14.
7. Chet Raymo, *The Soul of the Night* (New York: Prentice Hall, 1985), 46.
8. Gary Bennett, "Cosmic Origins of the Elements," *Astronomy*, Aug. 1988, 18.
9. Chet Raymo, Personal correspondence with author, September 20, 1990.
10. Gary Bennett, "Cosmic Origins of the Elements," *Astronomy*, Aug. 1988, 20.
11. Patrick Moore, *Armchair Astronomy* (New York: Norton, 1984), 128.
12. Chet Raymo, *The Soul of the Night* (New York: Prentice Hall, 1985), 102.
13. Louise B. Young, *The Blue Planet* (Boston: Little Brown, 1983), 266.

Chapter 11

1. Keith Naughton, "Killing Lincoln," *Bloomberg Businessweek*, Jan. 16-22, 2012, 57.

Chapter 12

1. William R. Palmer, *Why the North Star Stands Still* (Springdale, Utah: Zion National History Publishers, 2003), 25-29.
2. Tony Allan and Tom Lowenstein, *Gods of Sun and Sacrifice* (London: Duncan Baird Publishers, 2003), 47.

Chapter 13

1. Thich Nhat Hanh, *Peace Is Every Step* (New York: Bantam Books, 1991), 95-96.

Chapter 14

1. Malcolm Margolin, *The Ohlone Way* (Berkeley: Heyday Books, 2003), 117-122.
2. Henry David Thoreau, *Walden* (New York: Bramall House, 1951), 348.

Chapter 15

1. Jerome Walters, "The End of Birth," *New Age Journal*, Jan/Feb. 1994, 65.
2. Ibid., 65.
3. Lao Tzu, *The Way of Life*, trans. by Witter Bynner (New York: Capricorn Books, 1944), 43.
4. *Revelation* 11:18 (King James Version)
5. Psalm 104:24.
6. Calvin B. DeWitt, *Earth-Wise* (Grand Rapids, MI: CRC Publications, 1994), 52.
7. Thich Nhat Hanh, *The Heart of the Buddha's Teaching* (New York: Broadway Books, 1998), 126-127.

Chapter 16

1. Thich Nhat Hanh, *Being Peace* (Berkeley: Parallax Press, 1987), 65.
2. Matthew Arnold, *Essays in Criticism* (New York: MacMillan & Co. 1969), 173.
3. Seth Mydan's article "More than 2000 Die as Floods Swamp Towns in the Philippines," *New York Times*, Nov. 7th, 1991, A1,A8.
4. Helena Norberg-Hodge, "Economics, Engagement, and Exploitation in Ladakh," *Tricycle: The Buddhist Review*, Winter 2000, 115.
5. Eben Fodor, *Better Not Bigger* (Gabriola Island, B.C: new Society Publishers, 1999), 24.

Chapter 17

1. Christopher Williams, *Craftsman of Necessity* (New York: Vintage, 1974), 91.
2. B. Coburn, "Nepali Aama," *The Coevolutionary Quarterly*, Spring 1980, 104-105.

Chapter 18

1. David Abram, *Becoming Animal* (New York: Vintage Books, 2010).
2. Diane Ackerman, "Finding a Time Pool," *Audubon*, Jan/Feb, 2002, 49.
3. Henry David Thoreau, *Walden* (New York: Bramall House, 1951), 148.
4. Henry David Thoreau, *Walden* (New York: Bramall House, 1951), 128, 154.
5. Aldo Leopold, *A Sand County Almanac* (London: Oxford University Press, 1949), 96.
6. Joseph Cornell, *Listening to Nature* (Nevada City, CA: Dawn Publications, 1987), 42.
7. Sparlha Swaby, "The Venice Declaration: A Spiritual Imperative for Earth Care," *Earthlight*, Summer 2002, 6.
8. Martin Luther King Jr., *A Testament of Hope*, (New York: HarperCollins), 10, 13.
9. K.L. Reichelt, *Meditation and Piety in the Far East* (New York: Harper & Bros., 1954), 56.
10. *Old Farmer's Almanac*, New Hampshire: Yankee Publishing, Inc. Published annually.
11. D.T. Suzuki, *Zen Buddhism*, (New York: Doubleday, 1956), 3-4.
12. Walt Whitman, *Leaves of Grass* (New York: Paddington Press, 1970), 14.
13. Wendell Berry, "The Idea of a Local Economy," *Harper's Magazine*, April 2002, 16.
14. Richard Stevens, *Miracle Under the Oaks* (New York: Pocket Books, 1995), 16.
15. Psalm 26, verse 7 (King James Version).
16. Hara Akegarasu, "Oh New Year!," *Zen Notes*, Jan. 1975, 2.

CPSIA information can be obtained at www.ICGtesting.com
Printed in the USA
LVOW10s0520200813

348679LV00001B/52/P

9 781623 860004